BUCKEYE BUMPER CROPS

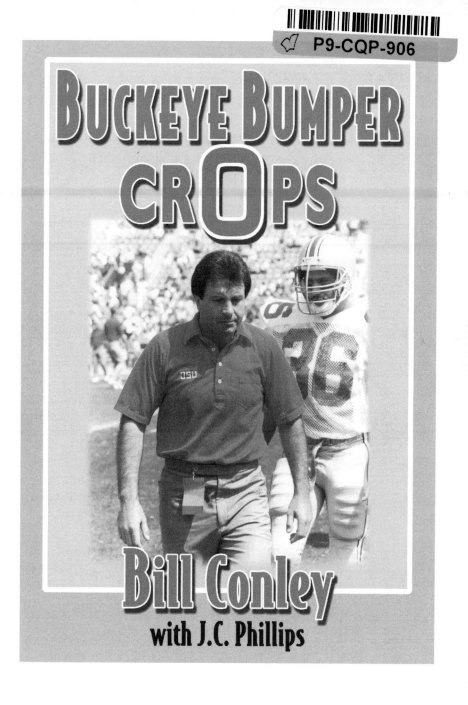

Bill Conley
with J.C. Phillips

Copyright © 2005, Bill Conley

ISBN 0-9773991-0-9

LCCN 2005908559

Printed in the United States of America

Contents

BIG HOLE FOR LEO—Halfback Leo Hayden (22) moves through a big opening made by his offensive line. Hayden had taken the handoff from Ron Maciejowski (18) as Tom Rabatin (64) tries to make the tackle. On the ground at right is Bill Conley (55) who had made a block.

That's me, No. 55, making a block in an intrasquad game.

London, Ohio, 43140, Thursday, May 30, 1974   50c Week by Carrier — Street Sale 10c Copy

Conley Named To Head London Grid Position

Bill Conley, an assistant football coach under Jim Bowlus since 1972, has been named to succeed him as head London High School grid mentor.

Conley, an Ohio State University graduate, was employed by the London Board of Education at a special session Wednesday evening.

More than 40 applicants expressed interest in the coaching position vacated by Bowlus, who retired to enter private business this year.

Conley has been head wrestling coach and will continue in that post for at least one year. He will be changing teaching positions, though. Conley has been teaching seventh and eighth grade history and will be moving to the high school to teach social studies, Supt. Charles Montgomery said.

Montgomery said as far as he knows the other assistant coaches who served under Bowlus will be staying on the staff under Conley.

The superintendent said the lengthy list of people interested in the coaching job was whittled down by eliminating some due to academic teaching positions open locally. Then interviews were conducted, including three Wednesday before the board's final decision.

"It will be a challenge to step into a program so well run by Bowlus," Conley said, adding that "with hard work from the coaching staff and the athletes, we'll be successful."

Conley graduated from Pleasant View High School near Grove City in 1968, where he competed in football and track.

As a freshman at Ohio State, Conley was a walk-on with the football team who landed a scholarship as a sophomore. He emerged as a four-year veteran of Woody Hayes' teams on the offensive line and specialty teams, surviving a Rose Bowl defeat from Stanford as well as a Big-Ten Championship and Co-Championship, and a National Championship.

Discussing his coaching philosophy, Conley said he places emphasis on conditioning, simplicity, discipline and sound execution.

Conley, the 23-year-old son of Mr. and Mrs. Eucker Conley of Ashland, Ky., lives in Columbus with his wife Deborah.

In other action, the board:

HIRED Herb Samuels, teacher at Deercreek, for summer maintenance work at the Somerford and Deercreek buildings. He will help with painting and other such work.

EMPLOYED library aides for the summer to help get the Primary Building books correctly catalogued according to Title I standards. Named were Deborah Gilbert, Rhonda Kacir and Judy Garringer.

HIRED Sara Crist, a graduate of Wittenberg University with a masters degree from Cincinnati, to teach a third-fourth grade combination class. She has three years of experience.

APPROVED attendance at two conferences, one for Montgomery to attend the Buckeye Assn. of School Administrators meeting this summer and the other for Deborah Gilbert and Judy Garringer to attend an educational conference.

Bill Conley

That's the story from the London, Ohio paper announcing my promotion to head coach at age 23.

Acknowledgments

I wish to acknowledge the contributions of a number of people whose guidance, assistance and support made this book possible:

- **Jack Park**, the nationally recognized Ohio State Football historian and friend, who helped verify statistical and biographical information.
- **Jeff Snook**, author and independent sports writer and friend, who gave advice and guidance in the early stages of this project.
- **My colleagues at MAX Sports Center**, especially **Dr. John Lombardo, Brad Cochran** and **Sheri Phipps,** for their support and encouragement of this endeavor.
- **George Lehner, Earle Bruce, Keith Byars** and **Dave Purdy,** my colleagues at 610 WTVN radio, with whom I do pre- and post-game college football analysis. Your support and guidance is appreciated beyond words.
- All the players, coaches and colleagues at The Ohio State University for the opportunity to be part of an outstanding and unique fraternity.

- All the outstanding high school coaches and administrators I've met and worked with on my recruiting odyssey across the United States and Canada.
- The various Ohio State alumni clubs I've had the opportunity and pleasure to address through the years.
- My sons, **Bill** and **Craig (in photo below),** for their understanding and support while their father pursued his dreams.
- **Bob, Paul** and **Dan,** my longtime friends and charter members of WDI.

Introduction

During his 17 years as an assistant football coach for the Ohio State Buckeyes, Bill Conley coached tight ends, linebackers, defensive ends and special teams for head coaches Earle Bruce, John Cooper and Jim Tressel. All-American and/or eventual NFL players he coached include Cris Carter, Thomas "Pepper" Johnson, Chris Spielman, Mike Vrabel, Andy Groom, B.J. Sander, Ben Hartsock, Darnell Sanders and Mike Nugent.

Conley coached teams that included the 2002 national champions, and others earning berths in numerous bowl games, including the Rose, Fiesta, Outback, Sugar, Citrus, Holiday, Hall of Fame and Cotton Bowls.

As the Buckeyes' recruiting coordinator in 1991 and 1992, and then from 1994 to 2004, Conley distinguished himself and gained national acclaim. Recognized by ESPN as the No. 1 college football recruiter in the country, Conley consistently brought high-impact or "franchise" players to Ohio State. A few of those players include Eddie George, Orlando Pace, Terry Glenn, Greg Bellisari, Andy Katzenmoyer, Chris Gamble, Nate Salley and Mike Nugent.

Conley is a graduate of The Ohio State University, where he was a member of three Big Ten championship teams, including the 1968 national championship team, under legendary head coach Woody Hayes. Conley earned a bachelor's degree in education from Ohio State, and a master's degree in administration from Wright State University.

In the spring of 2004, Conley retired from Ohio State and was named vice president at MAX Sports Center, a sports medicine and athletic performance institute in Columbus, Ohio. Today, he works to improve the skills of the nation's top athletes, while keeping his ears to the ground for coaches looking for that next franchise player. Along with being one of the nation's top motivational speakers, Conley is also a radio sports analyst for 610 WTVN in Columbus, Ohio.

Prologue

Imagine never going to the grocery store again, and not because you don't want to, but because you don't have to go. Instead, farmers and/or their representatives come directly to you, bringing with them not only the freshest, highest-quality products from which to choose, but the statistical data to support their claims to the superiority of a particular harvest. Such data in this instance would include levels of annual rainfall verses sunlight, mean air and soil temperatures, soil moisture and erosion charts, nutrients and additives, and information about pest infestations, to name a few.

Now imagine those same farmers hawking their crops to dozens of other potential customers like you, spawning a fierce and sometimes bitter competition among buyers. Imagine these efforts transcending growing seasons and becoming a perpetual process. This means if you let your guard down or divert your attention for just a moment, you stand the chance of losing a crop that is the envy of your family, your peers and your profession. Farmers commonly refer to exceptional harvests as "bumper crops."

That anecdote is an apt metaphor for the process of recruiting football players at the NCAA Division I level. It is a world where I made a living for nearly 20 years as an assistant coach at The Ohio State University under respected head coaches Earle Bruce, John Cooper and Jim Tressel. The farmers in this scenario are the parents, legal guardians, coaches, pastors or high school representatives of the nation's top recruits; the consumers are the hundreds of Division I football programs across the United States.

The average person hears about recruiting once a year, in early February when media and industry pundits chronicle, critique and classify how each of the nation's major universities—particularly those from well-known football schools, such as Ohio State—fared in a given year. Everyone seems to want to know whether a particular harvest (class of recruits, to continue our metaphor) will bear the sweet fruit that leads to a league championship or highly coveted national championship. The only other time most people hear about recruiting is when there are violations of the rules of conduct prescribed by the National Collegiate Athletic Association (NCAA), the governing body of college athletics.

This book, however, is not about rankings of recruiting classes, nor is it about the rule makers or breakers, or the seemingly bottomless pit of enablers, scoundrels and bloodsuckers that seem to plague college sports. This book isn't about the NCAA, although I will examine several key policies that have altered and evolved the state of recruiting. This book is about how recruiting is both an art and science, how it is part Picasso and part Freud, if you will. Ultimately, recruiting is about understanding human nature, and what it is that drives coaches and athletes to be part of and contribute to something greater than themselves. To fully comprehend my approach to recruiting you must first understand me. I am a teacher at heart, which is what I firmly believe a majority of coaches are at their core. My first job out of college was teaching middle school social studies in London, Ohio. I care deeply about people and their personal and professional development; I enjoy helping others succeed. My focus for 30 years has been on the development of football players as athletes and individuals. I am no different than other teachers, except that my classroom is the gridiron and my medium is Division I football, which is arguably one of the most exciting sporting and social phenomenon in North America.

Though the process of recruiting is important to understand, it's also important to point out that successful recruiters have their own approach, philosophy and skills they apply to their trade. It may be a stale remark, but what works for one doesn't necessarily work for another. Understanding an individual's inner motivations is vital to the process. So, too, is finding out who else is pivotal in his decision-making process and what will make him pull the trigger and attend your school. Each recruit I've ever encountered—and it probably numbers in the thousands—has a special story to tell . . . and what stories they are! How is it that this person rose above his contemporaries to reach a level of athletic achievement others only daydream about? Some experts would say it is a combination of genetics, hard work and a burning desire to excel that results in the creature called the Division I college football player. All I know is that the stories behind the young men I recruited to play at Ohio State are as different and unique as each individual, and I would be hard-pressed to categorize any of the young men I've coached. Recruiting is evolutionary, although it was a lower-profile, one-on-one endeavor prior to the mid-1980s. Before then, universities like Ohio State, Michigan, Notre Dame, Texas, Nebraska, Oklahoma, Alabama and USC were a lock to lure and hook a majority of the nation's top football talent. That was before the age of big-money sponsorships and television rights, and high-profile players leveraging their college experience to leave early for million-dollar paydays in professional football.

One-time, lesser-profile university football programs, such as Kansas State and Marshall, gained notoriety and prestige giving so-called second-tier players a chance to shine early and bolster their worth with professional scouts. Changes in the recruiting process also heightened competition among college recruiters as programs lost the luxury and routine of re-building programs by red-shirting players in key positions.

Recruiting is now a never-ending season, a high-stakes contest measured not only in wins and losses, but also the professional and personal fates of players and coaches alike. The pool of potential players hasn't changed drastically over the past 20 years; still only a tiny percent of all high school football players will play at the Division I level, and a small percentage of those will play at the professional level. What has changed is the process of recruiting. There literally has been an explosion of recruiting services and systems to track and rate top prospects, including recruiting magazines and the Internet. For example, Nike sponsors a series of annual Combines, where high school stars demonstrate their speed, agility, strength and football skills. Nike then posts national rankings of these players on its Web site. Talk about your cross-promotions! I'd like to have one-quarter of one percent of what those events must ultimately contribute to the company's bottom line.

Success in recruiting boils down to selling the merits of a particular program, that program's ability to perform as sold, and its value and track record of getting star athletes to the next level if they have the skill and desire. (Remember, only a small percentage of all Division I college football players will get a chance to play professionally, so the odds against most star athletes increase exponentially.) Watching these boiling points is the primary responsibility of the recruiting coordinator, whose greatest joy is that rare connection that brings mutual success for the athlete and the university's football program.

There is no greater feeling for a recruiting coordinator or recruiting coach than to land the ideal player for the most important position need. That perfect match is a great recruiting high. I know what academicians are groaning: "Isn't getting a college education and earning a degree more important than winning football games?" Let me say for the record that, yes, it is. I can only speak for Ohio State, which during my tenure gave its athletes every opportunity for success on and off the field. I know this from the perspective as a coach, and as a former player—a walk-on who earned a scholarship and completed not only his bachelor's degree, but also a master's degree. I know this practice was embraced, communicated and reiterated by all three coaches I was associated with during my time as a Buckeye assistant coach and recruiter. I also know that Woody Hayes, for whom I had the honor of playing, embraced and preached these tenets as well. A vast majority of coaches I know take personal pride in preparing their players not only for the battles they'll encounter on the football field, but conflicts they will encounter in life. As coaches, we believe that football lessons are life lessons, but we'll leave this debate for another arena as well.

Again, this book is about my experiences recruiting the cream of the national football crop, and trying to convince them to become Ohio State Buckeyes. Most were high-profile, highly acclaimed, nationally ranked players in high school that were aggressively pursued by the best collegiate programs. They could have played anywhere in the country. Ironically, several—including one Heisman Trophy winner—barely registered on the national recruiting radar and were initially overlooked by so-called recruiting experts, sophisticated recruiting services, scouts and those like me who made a living identifying real talent. Many of those athletes, however, possessed not only raw physical talent, but also a rare mental and emotional tenacity to become not only top collegiate athletes but franchise professional players as well.

I'll also try to explain the fickle, even schizophrenic nature of a business where I've spent my professional life. To that end and to help others, I've developed 11 fundamental rules of recruiting that I'm calling, *"Conley's Recruiting Commandments."* Explanations of these "Commandments" (listed at the end of this Prologue) will lead various chapters examining my personal experiences, and include vignettes of a few remarkable recruits I helped convince to play for Ohio State. Why 11 commandments, you may be asking. Well, the way I see it, if God were a coach in the Big Ten he/she would have given Moses 11 commandments. Seriously, my hope is that these observations, tips and stories will be compelling to fans and observers of both football and human nature, and a valuable resource to recruiters and the recruited by providing insight and guidance into the nuances of an interesting but frequently misunderstood process.

Ultimately, this book is about the young men who were given a chance to display their athletic skills on one of the most high-profile, and physically, emotionally and mentally demanding stages in collegiate sports—arguably in all of athletics—at The Ohio State University in Columbus, Ohio. What counts most is the fact that not only were these young men successful athletes, but their experiences have made most of them successful and respected citizens in their respective communities. The greatest fulfillment for any coach, including myself, is the belief that you have been a part of helping a young man mature. With that in mind, it is to all the young men that I have had the pleasure to recruit and coach that I dedicate this book. The emotional charge a coach gets from seeing the look in the face of one of his athletes after a big play, winning a league championship, capturing a national title or receiving a diploma is precious. I have been fortunate to experience many great moments in football, and to the young men who made it possible, all I can say is, "Thank you."

—Bill Conley

THE OHIO STATE UNIVERSITY
AREA OF STUDENT RELATIONS
INTERCOLLEGIATE ATHLETICS
ST. JOHN ARENA
410 WEST WOODRUFF
COLUMBUS, OHIO 43210

Office of Director

JuTy 14, 1970

AREA CODE 614
TELEPHONE: 293-2341

Dear Bill,

Next week I will send you a letter telling you when you are to report for practice. In the meantime, here are some thoughts I'd like to have you ponder:

1. More games will be won in the NEXT SIX WEEKS than during the rest of the season. CONDITIONING, and even more important, INDIVIDUAL IMPROVEMENT will make the difference.

2. Above all you must improve your SPEED. If you do so, we will be the fastest team in college football.

3. Don't work long, but DRIVE YOURSELF in every practice. If you haven't driven yourself, then you haven't practiced.

4. Make sure you don't get hurt in a FOOLISH ACCIDENT. This includes swimming accidents, water skiing accidents, highway accidents, Honda accidents, and industrial accidents.

5. HOW GREAT DO YOU WANT TO BE?

6. The DESIRE TO WIN is not as important as the DESIRE TO PREPARE TO WIN.

Your friend,

Woody Hayes

W. W. Hayes

WWH:sm

P.S.: How about taping this schedule to your bathroom mirror so you can see it the first thing every morning!

P.P.S.: NOVEMBER 21!

W.

Conley's Recruiting Commandments

   I. Recruiting is a numbers game.

  II. Identify the decision maker.

 III. Don't make false promises.

 IV. Ask the right questions.

  V. Pick the right host.

 VI. Make it tough to say "No."

VII. It's all academic.

VIII. Be able to look yourself in the mirror.

 IX. Home visits: Have your proverbial gun loaded.

  X. Make the high school coach your ally.

 XI. Parents must trust you.

Walk-On Happy
Bucks Surprise

By TOM KEYS, Citizen-Journal Sports Editor

If Bill Conley had a Pvt. before his name, he'd probably be the first guy in his outfit to volunteer for the job nobody else wanted.

Bill has, in fact, been volunteering his football services at Ohio State for more than a year. And should he continue to improve, the pleasant youngster from Pleasant View High may give fans from the Southwest section of the city something to cheer about.

AS IT IS the 5-10, 198-pound tight guard is drawing a few plaudits from both Woody Hayes and guard coach Earl Bruce. Not big ones . . . but they know Bill's around and the junior walk-on is now running No. 2 to Dick Kuhn.

"He's i m p r o v e d every day," Bruce said Wednesday after the second all-out scrimmage of the fall for the Buckeyes.

"He has a fine attitude and this has helped a great deal. His progress has been remarkable. He has a little problem now . . . on pass protection. But we're working on it and he'll learn."

THE BUCKS are thin at the position and Bill could find himself carrying a heavy load. Sophomore Larry Graf was slated for the No. 1 tight guard spot but when mono and other ailments grounded him, Kuhn was moved over from end. "But Conley was a starter in the spring game," reminded Bruce.

Reminding us that the 19-year-old junior is a walk-on, Woody said he was pleased with his progress "but we haven't given him a s c h o l a r s h i p yet." Maybe that'll come if he toughens up on pass protection.

KEYNOTES — The Red 1 unit was in for 69 plays and the Bucks (top defensive outfit) for 60 during a two-hour scrimmage Wednesday. "It was a pretty good one. No

Sports Illustrated, which has put the whammy on many an athletic team and hundreds of individuals, has aimed its guns this way. This week's SI (with Ole Miss' Archie Manning the cover boy), has picked OSU as the No. 1 team in the country. Rounding out the top 10 are Mississippi, Arkansas, Texas, Nebraska, Southern Cal, Notre Dame, Penn State, Michigan and Florida.

one was hurt and that's important. That's why I quit just a few minutes ahead of schedule," said Hayes . . . Two pro scouts, Bill Jobko of Atlanta and Jack Faulkner of New Orleans have been watching the Bucks. Both got special treatment as Bill played here and Faulkner, the ex-Denver coach, is a Miami grad . . . John Brockington "is our best back right now," praised Hayes, who also liked the work of Ron Maciejowski, Leo Hayden and s o p h o m o r e s Ross Moore, Gary Zetts. John Bledsoe and Rick Galbos, even t h o u g h the latter had three fumbles. Woody says speedster (9.4) Jimmie Lee Harris, who is breathing down the neck of two-year regular Bruce Jankowski, has "better hands at this stage than Paul Warfield. And he runs faster although Paul seemed to be a blur" . . . Sophomore Gary Lago of Ashtabula will handle the punting until Mike Sensibaugh returns to action.

Bill Conley
Working Walk-on

Conley's Recruiting Commandments

I. Recruiting is a numbers game.

Pursue six players for every available scholarship. Never assume that you are going to get every player that's offered a scholarship.

"Big Daddy" Dan Wilkinson was a late take recruit in 1991. We had missed out on some other defensive linemen, and fortunately we kept Dan on the list and stayed in contact with him. We didn't sign him until June of his senior year, and he not only went on to become an outstanding player for the Buckeyes, but also a first-round pick in the NFL draft in 1994. (Read more about Dan in chapter 7.)

My mother, Melba (Martin) Conley

My father, Eucker Conley

1

Read'n, Rit'n & Route 23

I was born at 6:46 A.M. on October 22, 1950 in Paintsville, Kentucky. I am the second son of Eucker and Melba Conley; my brother, Dean, is four years older. My mother always said that my birth brightened what was a gray, damp and dreary fall day, but isn't that what moms are supposed to say?

My father was one of 11 children in a long line of Conleys who hailed from Johnson County in the coal-rich hills of eastern Kentucky. In those days, most folks worked for the coal company, the railroad, the Commonwealth . . . or you ran moonshine. Often, people literally "moonlighted" at the latter trade, holding "respectable" jobs during the day. My father was a third generation C&O Railroad man and proud of it. But no, we did not operate a still in our backyard, as far as I know.

Many of my mother's relatives held state and local government jobs. For instance, my maternal grandfather, Marion Martin, was a deputy sheriff of Martin County in the 1920s. I'm told he encountered more than his share of 'shiners and other scallywags during his tenure. You see, in Kentucky—especially the eastern part of the state—most people love the Commonwealth but despise government. So it was no surprise that the law took a dim view of moonshiners, and vice versa.

While spelled differently, my father shared a name with a popular card game of the time, so maybe it was no coincidence that recreational activities were a big part of my early childhood years. Baseball, horseshoes, basketball and fishing were my primary pursuits from childhood into my early teens. This makes some sense because most Kentuckians have three primary passions: God, basketball and thoroughbred horse breeding and racing, and not necessarily in that order. Football was a stepchild activity there back then, something kids did to pass time between baseball and basketball seasons. Interestingly enough, I did not even play organized football until I was 16 and a junior in high school.

So, how did a kid who cut his teeth playing everything but football wind up making it his game of choice, and ultimately his vocation? I was nine when my parents split, and my mother responded to that event by making a pilgrimage thousands of Kentuckians were making at that time. She packed up our belongings and we drove north on U.S. Route 23 toward Columbus, Ohio. I still find amusing the old joke about how school children in Kentucky learn the three "R's," which stand for "Read'n, Rit'n and Route 23."

You may snicker, but Ohio was a land of opportunity during the automotive and steel industry boom of the 1950s and

1960s. At that time the proverbial Rust Belt was still a well-oiled machine and showed no signs of corrosion. The economy was so strong in the Buckeye State that my mother was encouraged to move by two of her brothers, who found steady, decent-paying jobs. So, she, my brother and I performed the "Route 23 Two Step" and moved to Ohio. She eventually landed a job as a beautician, and we settled on Columbus' west side, better known as The Hilltop. In addition to its economic prowess, Ohio also was a virtual breeding ground for football—the birthplace of professional football and home to the Pro Football Hall of Fame. People in Ohio are as passionate about football as people in Kentucky are about basketball and horses. I quickly learned the flames of football burn even hotter in Columbus, a town that then and now lives and dies with the fate of its Ohio State Buckeyes. To say Buckeye fanatics make normal fanatics look tame is an understatement; the only way to truly experience Buckeye mania is to attend a home game some crisp fall Saturday, and make your way through a literal maze of tailgaters in everything from motor homes to mopeds.

So there I was, a Kentucky native living in Buckeye country. One way for any "new kid" to make his mark and ward off peer predators is to excel in sports. I was a decent baseball player, which enabled me to make friends quickly and survive my middle school years. Even then, football was just something my friends and I did in the backyard to pass time, and expend some adolescent energy. I still did not even consider it a serious activity, let alone something that would ultimately consume my adult life.

I attended Pleasant View High School (which today is a middle school) and was quite happy finding relative success playing catcher on a pony league baseball team—I didn't even play baseball for our high school. Then my friend Roger Cordle got the bright idea of trying out for the football team the summer before our junior year in 1966. Well, guess who he persuaded to try out with him? That's right, yours truly. So, in the "if-your-friend-jumps-off-the-bridge-will-you?" tradition, I decided to try out for the football team. The rest is history, as they say. I discovered I had quite an aptitude for the sport, earning a starting position as a linebacker my junior year, and then playing both linebacker and offensive guard my senior year. I would earn varsity letters both years. Despite quick success and the attention it brings, it wasn't until I attended my first college football game by luck of the draw that I even considered playing a sport beyond high school.

On a Saturday morning after a mid-season game my senior year in 1967, head coach Don Eby called the team together and said he had an extra ticket for that afternoon's Ohio State football game. He conducted an impromptu drawing to see who would accompany him, and I won. To this day, I still vividly remember the afternoon of that game like it was yesterday—the pungent-sweet aroma of charcoal, bratwurst and beer as we walked amid a thundering sea of scarlet and gray-clad fans entering the archway of historical Ohio Stadium. I was 17 years old and making my first trip to the Horseshoe, as Ohio Stadium is known because of its unique architecture. Once inside, I could not absorb enough of the rumble caused by more than 80,000 people. My head was spinning in the spectacle and noise, which my pounding heart echoed. I've been to many stadiums for many games over the past 35 years—including the 2003 national championship game in Tempe, Arizona, when the Buckeyes defeated the Miami Hurricanes in one of the most exciting football games in history—and still nothing compares with game day at Ohio State. I still get chills and goosebumps when "The Best Damned Band In The Land" marches out of the closed end of the stadium. Only those who have been there can truly appreciate it. I've had Michigan fans tell me Wolverine games pale in comparison, even though Michigan Stadium now holds 111,000 people—now that's a compliment!

Back to the game: It was a bright and hot, late September day, and the Buckeyes were playing the University of Arizona. Perennial powerhouses in the Big Ten, the Buckeyes were struggling that year, so much so that airplanes circling the stadium were pulling banners that read: "Fire Woody." The "Woody" these signs were referring to was none other than *the* Woody Hayes, the famous and fiery head coach of the Buckeyes. The same Woody Hayes whose career record was 238-72-10, and who would win four national championships (five if you count the one given by the National Football Foundation in 1970) and 13 Big Ten titles. His teams played in eight Rose Bowls, and he produced three Heisman Trophy winners and 56 All-Americans. Yes, that Woody. Still that year there were some who thought the "Old Man" was getting past his prime, and should be put out to pasture. The one consistent with some Ohio State fans is a lack of consistency, at least when it comes to their affections.

Ohio State lost that particular game, 14-7, and Woody Hayes would keep his job, but the event was an epiphany for me. I decided that day that I wanted to play football in college and I wanted to play for Ohio State. The sights, the sounds and the emotions of that day intoxicated me; I wanted to hear the roar of the crowd as I ran onto that hallowed playing field. Like a Bowery bum in search of a drink, I wanted more and would not be satisfied until I got it.

Now, this may have been 1967, but at 5 feet 10 inches and 172 pounds, I was not a prototypical linebacker or offensive guard in Division I football, let alone Ohio State. I probably should have gotten the hint, as I was never recruited by Ohio State, but no one could tell me differently. I had already decided I would "walk-on" that next summer after graduating high school, and try to make the 1968 team. Little did I know what a special year that would be as Woody Hayes would lead the Buckeyes to a 10–0 record, and the Big Ten and national championships. It was the year of the "Super Sophomores," and names such as Rex Kern, Jack Tatum, Jim Stillwagon and Jim Otis would become household names and living legends that are still revered to this day by Buckeye fans.

A combination of financial aid and student loans gave me the necessary funds to attend Ohio State. I had no lofty expectations for football, and already decided if it did not work out, I'd still be able to get a good education like my brother, Dean, who would finish his bachelor's degree in political science the following year. Dean also served in the Reserve Officers Training Corps, and enlisted in the U.S. Navy as a lieutenant after graduating. After his Navy stint, Dean landed several jobs in and around the political scene in Columbus, the state's capital. In the late 1970s through the 1980s, Dean ran for and was elected to six consecutive terms as an Ohio state representative. Although our politics are quite different—Dean's a Democrat and I'm a Republican—I helped him on several campaigns and the experience tightened our relationship. Dean is now retired, but

I am still very proud of his accomplishments in the "real world," as it were.

Back to my freshman year at Ohio State. The reality of my particular situation hit me square in the face when at the first pre-season practice for freshmen, there were more than 100 walk-ons. These were all guys like me, guys who were relatively successful high school athletes who dreamed of continuing their athletic careers by becoming Ohio State Buckeyes. I am quite sure all of us had deer-in-the-headlights expressions on our faces as we were virtually ignored by coaches and "scholarship" players. In case you didn't know it, walk-ons are essentially cannon fodder for most college teams; they are the lowest of the low, the dust that dirt discards. And while Ohio State is a university of vast resources, we were given the worst equipment and worn out practice uniforms . . . I think even our jockstraps were pre-owned! The bottom line is that you either got tough or you got out, and I was either too dumb or too stubborn to follow the latter path. Within the first week, more than half of the walk-on players in this particular class were dismissed after coaches learned they recorded unacceptably low scores on college entrance exams. Setting a test-score threshold gave the coaches a legitimate reason to cull our numbers. More walk-on players would "disappear" that year and the next as the physical and psychological demands intensified. By the time I was a senior, only three other walk-on players that started with me remained on the team. Who was it that said misery loves company? Nonetheless, there we were and seemingly all too proud to take the abuse.

It never was my destiny to be a high-profile, franchise player like Rex Kern, Archie Griffin or Eddie George. No. I was a too small, too slow of a kid who was motivated by pride and fear, and powered by passion and emotion. To say I was naïve is an understatement. Nevertheless, I dedicated myself in the off-seasons, and took to a weight-training regiment that helped put 236 pounds of muscle on my nearly 6-feet-tall frame by my senior season. I was a scout team player my freshman and sophomore years, but impressed the coaches enough that I earned a full-ride scholarship my second year, which is something I'm still quite proud of given my economic standing at that time. My junior and senior years I earned starting positions on special teams, and was a back-up offensive guard. It may not seem like much to you, but I realized my dream each and every time I sprinted onto that field before games, or when stepping out for a special teams play. I got to feel what it was like to be on the receiving end of the attention and cheers of tens of thousands of fans. It's heady, emotional stuff, and more than I ever imagined it would be.

Maybe you're asking, "What does any of this have to do with recruiting?" Well, everything, in my book. You see, as someone who had to scratch and bite to make the team and earn a scholarship, I saw how the art of recruiting works from the ground up. I got to observe and understand not only coaching tactics and techniques, but also variations and extremes of player personalities. I experienced that special bond of trust that occurs between players and coaches. Woody Hayes was the unmatched master of reading player personalities and motivating individuals. Still, Woody wasn't my only mentor. Consider this list of assistant coaches who were at Ohio State when I played, and then went on to other high-profile positions and national acclaim, including:

- **Earle Bruce** (my offensive line coach; took over as Ohio State's head coach after Woody, following head coaching stints at the University of Tampa and Iowa State University; he also was my first college-level boss);
- **Dave McClain** (head coach at Wisconsin);
- **Lou McCullough** (athletic director at Iowa State);
- **Rudy Hubbard** (head coach at Florida A & M);
- **Lou Holtz** (head coach at Notre Dame and the University of South Carolina);
- **Dick Walker** (assistant coach with the Pittsburgh Steelers during their Super Bowl-winning runs in the late 1970s and early 1980s);
- **Bill Mallory** (head coach at the University of Colorado and Indiana University);
- **Ralph Staub** (head coach at the University of Cincinnati);
- **George Chaump** (head coach at Marshall University and the U.S. Naval Academy, and quarterbacks coach for the Tampa Bay Buccaneers);
- **Hugh Hindman** (athletic director at Ohio State—known as the man who fired Woody Hayes after the now-infamous "Clemson incident" in the 1978 Gator Bowl); and
- **Glenn "Tiger" Ellison** (my freshman coach and inventor of an offensive scheme that became the popular "Run and Shoot").

Because he was my position coach, Earle Bruce had a tremendous influence on me. Like Woody, Earle was cut from the "tough-but-fair" cloth of coaching, meaning he had a way of dressing you down and dressing you up in the same, profanity rich sentence. Earle Bruce demanded excellence no matter what you were doing on the field, whether you had the ball or were downfield blocking. An interesting incident at one practice my freshman year told me that Earle was merely a dedicated disciple of Woody.

During sessions where our offense would "time up" plays for the upcoming game, Woody was the only coach on the playing surface. The assistants, however, knew not to stray too far because if a problem arose, Woody usually placed the blame on them rather than the players. Well, on this particular play, an offensive guard missed a key block, and Woody went berserk. He immediately turned to Earle and began verbally lambasting him, his forefathers and descendents in front of God and the team. OK, while I am exaggerating the depth of Woody's familial critique, Earle knew better than to say anything at the time. Instead, he stood silent with his hands pressed firmly in the back pockets of his pants, backing away from the spitting coach with his head down. I guess that was wrong posture for Earle to assume, as the team learned the following day that Woody had ordered equipment manager John Bozick to sew shut the back pants pockets of all assistant coaches. Don't feel sorry for Earle; he could be just as tough as Woody if something didn't go the way he thought it should.

Though I worked with Earle Bruce every day, each of the men I mentioned previously played an essential part in my decision to become a coach after earning my degree. I like to believe that the person and coach I strive to be is a reflection and tribute to the special mentors I had in life. As a coach, you hope you can influence athletes on and off the field, that your passion for what is merely a game instills in them a passion for life.

You also hope that elements of what you were taught by others live in what you teach, thus immortalizing those individuals.

These words, for instance, are an homage to the coaches that fueled that passion in me, a passion that continues burning quite brightly, I must say. The following statement made by Woody Hayes still rings in my head: "You never stay the same. You either get better or worse everyday." I can only hope I am making my mentors proud.

As I stated before, I was lucky to be part of the 1968 national championship team. Although I did not get an opportunity to contribute to the team's on-field success, I like to believe my efforts and performance on the freshman and scout teams helped strengthen our program and bolster the performance of the starters.

I will never forget one particular summer practice prior to the start of that year. I was playing linebacker on the scout team, and the coaching staff was putting in our option offense. Jim Otis, the All-Big Ten, and future All-American and St. Louis Cardinals standout, was playing fullback, and on this play the quarterback faked a handoff into the line. Thinking Jim had the ball and wanting to prove myself, I met him at the line of scrimmage and orchestrated one of the best "form fit" tackles I ever had as a player. Not having the ball, Jim didn't hit the line with his usual aggression and power, and I was able to make what I thought was a great tackle. Then I heard the screaming:

"Conley, why the hell did you tackle Otis?"

It was Woody, and he was giving me one of those looks that made some players soil their pants or quit on the spot. I did neither, but also did not move a muscle.

"I thought he had the football, sir," I squeaked out.

"Well, you're damned right you did. It was one hell of a fake," Woody smirked, recognizing the efforts of quarterback Rex Kern.

Man, was I relieved!

Telling that story means I also have to tell about the time when Jim did have the ball on a dive play. The last thing I remember is meeting him at the line, and feeling his helmet catch me under the chin before being knocked unconscious. I learned later that he drove and carried me for 10 yards before tripping over me. At another practice that year, Woody called for the second team offense, and I thought I'd at least have a chance to prove my worth. Wrong. You see, the backup fullback was none other than John Brockington, another future All-Big Ten and All-American player, and first-round draft pick and legendary running back for the Green Bay Packers. What was frightening was the fact that Brockington was actually faster than Otis, and had a way of using his knees as weapons as he ran. It still hurts to think about it!

Before you start feeling sorry for me or thinking I was not very bright for putting up with this abuse, I wasn't a blocking dummy my entire college career. I got to put a few licks on real opponents in real games. One of my most memorable moments came on the kick-off receiving team against Michigan my senior season in 1971. It's important to point out, at that time, players could still "legally" block below the waist. Having stated this, I remember running down the field, diving at an opposing player, and then hearing a loud, almost sickening groan as I took him out of the play. A few minutes later I saw that player on the Michigan sidelines with his shoulder pads off and walking on crutches. In hindsight I feel bad about the injury, knowing I must have gotten his knees, but at the time, I have to admit, I was proud to contribute to what would be a losing cause that year. No, I've never taken the time to find out whom that player was, but I obviously still think about him. Still, that's the game of football, and we all accept the potential risks and rewards when we suit up. By the way, that year we went 6–4, in what was a less than average but rebuilding year for the Buckeyes.

Being part of the 1968 Buckeye team was amazing beyond words, but to be twice blessed this way is indescribable. Serving on the coaching staff of the undefeated 2002 Buckeye team was a moment of distinction personally and professionally. It was distinctive because not only did I play a lead role in recruiting many of the players on that squad, I also contributed to their athletic and personal development as a position coach. I was privileged to observe a rare confluence of personalities moving in concert toward a goal. I'll be the first to admit that the Miami Hurricanes had some better individual athletes—just consider how many of the young men from that roster are now playing in the NFL. None of that mattered that day in Arizona in January 2003 because we had the better team, and the better team won that double-overtime contest. But we'll discuss that season and that game in greater detail in another chapter.

I graduated from Ohio State in the late spring of 1972 with a bachelor's degree in comprehensive social studies. To this day, that accomplishment overshadows anything I ever accomplished on the gridiron; the pride I saw in my mother's eyes told me that I had done something special. In mid-June, I signed a contract to begin teaching in the fall at Crestview High School near Ashland, Ohio. I would never spend a day at that job, however, and instead would get a lesson in the power of Buckeye connections. In mid-June, I received a call from the late Jim Bowlus, who at that time was head coach at London High School in London, Ohio, a football-rich rural community about 15 miles west of Columbus. During our brief phone conversation, I immediately could tell why he was a friend and contemporary of Woody Hayes. Bowlus was an irresistible force of a personality, and he was determined to have me change my plans and come work at London. To be polite, I agreed to visit the school, although I still intended to honor my contract with Crestview. Well, Bowlus' full-court press only intensified when I met him in person. At one point during our meeting, Bowlus excused himself from the room. He returned 15 minutes later and handed me a typed letter of resignation addressed to the superintendent of Crestview, a teaching contract for London, and a supplemental contract to serve as an assistant coach for football and head JV baseball coach. Believe me, I understood quite well that Buckeye forces were at work here, and besides, Bowlus had a great reputation as a teacher and coach, so adding him to my list of mentors would be a wise move. After taking a few moments to weigh my options, I decided to sign both letters. I left that meeting and enjoyed the remainder of the summer, preparing to begin my first gig as a professional teacher and coach. It's important to point out that London is the hometown of Dick LeBeau, a former Buckeye and Hall of Fame player for the Detroit Lions, and longtime NFL coach. It's also the hometown of Bill Hackett, Jr., who played linebacker for the Buckeyes and was one of my teammates.

I had planned to work under Bowlus for a couple years as an assistant to enrich my resume, increase my football knowledge and hone my coaching skills before pursuing a head coaching job. But like my short-lived job at Crestview High School, this plan too would change. During the late winter of my second year at London, I received a call from Jim Gladden, who was head coach at Hernando County High School, located north of Tampa, Florida. I did not personally know Gladden, who I learned got my name from a list I signed while attending a coaching clinic in Louisville, Kentucky, earlier that year. At that time, a massive influx of people to Florida from the north created a demand for more teachers and coaches.

Anyway, Gladden had a proposition that interested me. He wanted me to come to Florida and serve as his assistant for one year, and then take over as head coach at a new high school being built in the area. I must admit the thought of becoming a head coach at age 24, and getting away from Ohio winters appealed to me, so I agreed to visit Gladden during spring break to talk some more. The climate and facilities were more than I expected and my interest peaked. Also appealing was the thought of working with some of the nation's best football talent. At that time, Florida was just beginning to emerge as hotbed of "skill" players.

Driving back to Ohio, I had already made up my mind to make the move, or so I thought. Unexpected news awaited my arrival in London, which would again disrupt what I believed were best-laid plans. What I learned was that, during the break, Bowlus announced his retirement after 25 years of coaching and teaching. So, with youthful arrogance and a feeling that I had nothing to lose on my side—I already had a job offer in Florida—I applied for the London job not really expecting to get it. Fate played the joker once again, and I was named head coach at London High School in May 1973; at age 23, I was now the youngest head high school football coach in Ohio.

The reality of my situation—that I had only been part of organized football for seven years—came crashing down on me that spring. An overwhelming fire and fear consumed me, and the words, actions and lessons of my mentors spun in my head like a whirlpool. I spent the next few months talking with older, more experienced coaches, grabbing opportunities at clinics, meetings and social outings to pick their brains for morsels of information and guidance. I literally learned as I plodded through summer conditioning and practices, as well as first season when we went 6–2–2. I continued this voracious quest leading up to my second season at London. That year we went 10–0 and finished the season ranked No. 2 in Ohio. I would spend another two years as head coach of London, amassing a record of 30–8–2 before leaving teaching and coaching for one year to work for Ashland Chemical in Cleveland. Landing the Ashland Chemical position offered me a great opportunity to get some valuable business experience. Besides, the pay was much more attractive than what teachers were earning in the late 1970s. Despite it all, I missed coaching more than I anticipated.

The following year, in 1979, I accepted a teaching position and head coaching job at Groveport High School in Groveport, Ohio (a Columbus suburb), where I remained for three years and had a 15–14–1 record. In 1982, I had an opportunity to move to Middletown High School in Middletown, Ohio.

Middletown was and is to this day a sports-rich and sports-rabid community. It's the hometown of star athletes, such as basketball player Jerry Lucus and Olympic track star Todd Bell, the man who broke Jesse Owens long jump record. Middletown also was where Tiger Ellison, who was then an assistant coach at Ohio State, staked his claim to fame in coaching with his inventive and dynamic offense. I literally walked into a goldmine of athletic talent, inheriting a class of juniors that included several All-American high school and eventual college and professional stars, such as Cris Carter, Sean Bell, Dwight Smith, Al Milton and Sonny Gordon. In my two years at Middletown, we amassed a record of 15–5, going 9–1 the second year and missing the state playoffs by a quirk of state standings. Our only loss the second season was to the eventual state champion, Cincinnati Princeton, who beat us 23–22. That game alone featured 11 players who would eventually play Division I college football. I had never seen as much speed in one place at one time.

I could have stayed and retired from Middletown and been quite satisfied. The dedication and work ethic of the players and support of the families were unmatched in my experience to date. Yet our success attracted not only statewide but national attention, as did a number of players for which we had Division I universities competing. The attention by recruiters and the media also did something else; it renewed my relationship with Earle Bruce, who was hired in early 1979 as head coach at Ohio State. You see, Ohio State was one of a number of schools vying for our top players, and it would eventually get Carter, Smith, Bell and Gordon. The Buckeyes would also get me. How, you may be asking. You see, Woody began and Earle continued a tradition of filling at least one assistant coaching position at Ohio State with someone from the ranks of Ohio high schools. Both coaches believed the combination of raw game and people knowledge gleaned at the high school level was essential to building a successful college program. Most high school coaches, including myself, dreamed of getting such a call, but we all understood and accepted the fact that more than mere coaching talent had much to do with just who got tapped. Yes, the coaching profession is as political as any other. I was lucky. I remember shaking with excitement when I received the call from Earle Bruce in the mid-summer of 1984, asking if I'd consider coming to Ohio State as one of his assistants. Although my heart was torn, there was no way I could reject the opportunity to return to my alma mater and work for my former position coach. I accepted the job and arrived at summer practice just as a new crop of freshmen was arriving. It was a class that not only included three of my former Middletown standouts, but also another young man by the name of Chris Spielman. By the way, Earle made me coach of the linebacker corps. (On a side note, another new assistant coach hired a few months before me in 1983 was Jim Tressel, the current head coach at Ohio State. Tressel was hired to replace Dom Cappers, who left the Buckeyes to be a coach with the Philadelphia Stars of the United States Football League.)

I will always be thankful that I began my coaching career in the high school ranks, where the head coach also plays the role of parent, mentor, psychologist, sociologist, janitor, athletic trainer and marketing agent. I learned first hand that the X's and O's of football are a minor part of the game, and that football, like life, is more about managing personalities and events. Football games are merely one act of this drama we call life, and the primary facet of that act is recruiting. The essence of recruiting is not only filling roles within the team dynamic, but also making sure each of those parts works as a successful unit. The primary difference between coaching in high school (public not parochial) and coaching in college is that in high school, you build a team with the players you have, and in college you recruit players to build the team. Sounds simple, doesn't it? I can say from experience that it is not easy. The process of recruiting is like putting together a jigsaw puzzle; many pieces appear to fit, but only a few actually do match. And like a jigsaw puzzle, recruiting takes time, patience and an ability to see the big picture within the various pieces.

Conley's Recruiting Commandments

II. Identify the decision maker.

Get to know on a personal level the primary influence or decision maker in the life of each recruit, if it is not the athlete himself. It's usually a parent, but it can be another relative, a friend, a coach or a pastor, to name a few.

Ohio State missed a chance at landing tight end Kellen Winslow Jr., who went on to be an All-American at the University of Miami and a first-round draft pick of the Cleveland Browns. The decision maker was Kellen's mother, even though she lived on the East Coast and Kellen lived on the West Coast. Unfortunately, by the time we realized this it was too late, and we would ultimately face Kellen in the 2002 national championship game.

That's me during my stint as head coach at Groveport High School in the early 1980s. You gotta love the pants!

Recruiting 101

*The good, the bad, the ugly . . . and the
downright mind-boggling*

The foundation of successful college football programs is recruiting. It is impossible to be a superior team with inferior
players. There is no magic to the X's and O's of college football,
only how big, fast and skilled those X's and O's are on the field.
The surest way to shorten your college coaching career is by
thinking that you are going to out-think, out-plan and outsmart
that fellow on the other sideline. There gets to be a point where
there are only so many offensive plays and so many defensive
schemes to run. Only when the talent level is equal or near
equal does the strategic part of football become important.
Many coaches would be better off spending more of their time
and effort on recruiting players than trying to outwit the enemy.

The best head coaches in football are those who know the
value of recruiting. Many of those coaches are the best "sales

people" on the staff. They have a magical way of convincing parents and recruits that the university, football program and coaching staff they represent is superior to any others. Former Buckeye head coach Woody Hayes was an unrivaled master at recruiting. It was at the feet of Woody where I learned the importance of identifying the key decision maker in the life of any recruit, and to focus my efforts on that individual or group of people.

Archie Griffin, college football's only two-time Heisman Trophy winner, readily admits that Woody spent more time with his parents than with him. Woody instinctively knew that if he could sell the program and the university to Archie's mother and father, he would land Archie. Many people know what happened next in this story:

Between 1973 and 1975, Archie broke nearly all the Ohio State rushing records on his way to becoming the only two-time winner of the Heisman Trophy, which is awarded annually to "The Outstanding College Football Player of the Country." He was a three-time All America selection—in 1973, 1974 and 1975. He also was named Most Valuable Football Player in the Big Ten for two straight years, thereby becoming only the second athlete in history to accomplish this feat. A two-year Buckeye captain, Archie was named College Football Player of the Year by both *United Press International* and by the *Sporting News*. He is also the first athlete in Ohio State's history to have his number retired. In addition to numerous other honors, *College Football News* ranked Archie 15th on a list of the 100 Greatest Players of All-Time.

Here's what Woody Hayes had to say about Archie Griffin: "He's a better young man than he is a football player, and he's the best football player I've ever seen." A first-round draft pick of the Cincinnati Bengals in 1976, Archie played for eight seasons before retiring in 1984. That year, he was hired as an assistant in the Ohio State Athletic Department, becoming an associate director of athletics in 1994. In 2004, Archie was named president and CEO of The Ohio State University Alumni Association.

When it comes to recruiting, not everyone has the instincts and charisma of Woody Hayes. If a head coach knows he doesn't have the personality to be a great one-on-one salesperson, it is imperative he hire assistant coaches who can fill that void. It is equally important for him to hire a recruiting coordinator who can organize, plan and sell the entire recruiting process. Head coaches who ignore the necessity of a strong recruiting program are doomed to failure.

The recruiting process has changed dramatically over the past 30 years. Continual alterations of the rules by the NCAA bureaucracy, along with modern technology (especially the Internet) have made the entire recruiting process complicated and confusing. Consider the fact that it wasn't long ago university alumni were permitted to take recruits and parents out to dinner, transport them to college games, make unlimited telephone calls, write letters, and so on. In other words, alumni could do almost anything short of adopting the recruit and his family. As you might suspect, these practices got out of control to the point where money was flowing freely from alumni to recruits, and their relatives or guardians. Anytime there is an abuse of the rules the NCAA, in theory, steps in to halt the wrongdoings. Unfortunately, the NCAA believes making new rules, instead of enforcing existing rules, is the key to compliance. Many times the

NCAA, due to a lack of political courage, ignores some of the most flagrant rule violations and violators. The NCAA often turns its back on major programs that historically break the rules and, as a result, the institution itself—the NCAA—loses respect among its own members. But this book isn't about blasting the NCAA because that would be a book in itself.

One rule that has changed forbids alumni from contacting recruits via the telephone, letters or by e-mail. The initial intention of such correspondence was for colleges and universities to get their academic message across to recruits by building a rapport with successful alumni. As you may suspect, this got out of hand. Some schools began using former athletes, or those alumni who were famous entertainers or politicians to make first contact with recruits. For example, the University of Michigan used alumnus and former President Gerald Ford in its recruiting process. Tell me that getting a call or letter from a former president of the United States wouldn't influence the decision of someone who is age 17 or 18. Please don't misunderstand me, as those activities were acceptable and well within NCAA rules at that time, and if President Ford had been an Ohio State graduate, we would have used him as well. Unfortunately, former presidents from Ohio died well before the advent of the phenomenon that is modern day college football.

Universities were once permitted to send posters to recruits. These glossy, full-color posters usually consisted of stadium photographs, action shots from games or something unique about the university to sell a recruit. For example, Vanderbilt University once distributed a poster of then-popular and attractive country singer Barbara Mandrel dressed as a cheerleader and posing with the football team. Other universities that were renowned for passing prowess distributed posters of their quarterback and receivers posed with jet fighter airplanes. Many of these posters were quite unique and very creative. One of the ideas we came up with at Ohio State was to send posters of players from specific geographical areas. For example, if we had six players from South Florida, we put their images on a poster and distributed it to high school coaches and recruits from that area to promote the Ohio State/Florida connection. We did this for recruits in Ohio as well. One year, we featured All-American wide receiver Cris Carter surrounded by other Buckeye players from southwest Ohio, and distributed it throughout the Dayton and Cincinnati region. (On a side note, I still consider myself fortunate to be Cris' coach when he played at Middletown High School, and that I got to witness this young athlete develop into the Hall of Fame–caliber player he became with the Minnesota Vikings.)

Once again, overzealousness by some alumni led to a rule change. The straw that broke the camel's back came in 1984, when Clemson University distributed life-sized posters of refrigerators to promote highly touted senior William "The Refrigerator" Perry. Yes, it's true. So many colleges and universities complained to the NCAA that they had a disadvantage because they couldn't afford to produce such a large poster. This resulted in a total ban on posters, and a restriction on the color, size, weight and content of recruiting mail.

Official visits by recruits to college campuses is a topic that has been hotly debated through the years. The NCAA rules governing such visits have been subject to the most alterations over the past 20 years. At one time, recruits could take "official" visits to the same campus more than once. Because the recruiting process lasted well into the spring, the frequent visits became a nightmare for college coaches. After the first visit, the recruit usually came back to campus just for the social aspect of the college experience. During subsequent visits—even though the recruit may have made a final decision—the recruit wanted to soak up more of college life and socialize (read: party) with players and other students.

Once again, complaints of abuses led to change. Today, a recruit is limited to one official visit per institution, and they must be completed by the beginning of February each year. College coaches, athletic directors and presidents celebrated these changes. Now, a prospect is limited to five official visits (which could easily change to four or even three) with signing occurring in February. Not long ago, a recruit would sign a conference letter, which limited him to one school in that conference, but not a national letter. A national letter of intent, which indicated a recruit's final choice, was signed several weeks later.

Even though the official recruiting visit is highly regulated, the process is a potential nightmare for college football coaches. The entire time a recruit is on an official visit, the coach is concerned about potential problems, while at the same time trying to "sell" the recruit on the qualities of a particular university. It's no surprise that potential scandals involving underage drinking, drugs and sex continually plague coaching staffs and university administrators. Unfortunately, because human nature is fallible and unpredictable, for the 48 hours a recruit is on campus for an official visit, coaching staffs have their fingers crossed and their eyes wide open for trouble. They also breathe a sigh of relief when a recruit and his parents go home without incident.

As recruiting coordinator at The Ohio State University, I always believed it was my duty to not only organize the recruiting weekends, but also monitor the activities of the recruits and their parents or guardians. The job is massive, and entails booking flights, arranging lodging, planning meals, securing player hosts, setting academic and athletic appointments and giving tours of the campus, to name a few. If it weren't for the efforts of recruiting assistant Sherrie Kauffman and assistants such as John Hill, it would have been an impossible task, because I also had recruits and recruiting area of my own to monitor on top of my regular coaching duties. I even went as far as staying in the hotel where we housed the recruits for the weekend in case any issues arose. And yes, issues always arose.

I like to tell the story about the telephone call I received at 2:30 A.M. one weekend from the mother of a recruit, requesting that I come down to her hotel room because there was a "major problem." As I hurried down the hallway toward the elevator, I could only imagine what was going on. One thing was for certain, the woman on the other end of the line was quite distraught. When I arrived at her room, I was astonished to find out that her 19-year-old daughter, who she brought along on the trip, not only went into labor in the hotel room, but also gave birth to what seemed to be a healthy baby girl. After pacing for only a moment, I called the front desk and urged that they summon medical help immediately. Please remember that my college degrees are in education, not medicine. Even though I survived the birth of both of my sons, these situations still throw you for a loop, especially when you're focused on selling a university to a high school recruit. Fortunately, this story has a happy ending, as mother and child . . . and grandma . . . were all just fine.

As I recall the anxiety, surprise and then joy associated with that story, it triggers thoughts of one of the saddest days of my life, and a true tragedy for the Buckeye family:

A ringing telephone once again wakened me from a deep sleep. Glancing at the clock, I noticed it was 4 A.M. To quote current Buckeye head coach Jim Tressel, "Nothing good happens after 10 P.M." It was December 12, 1993, and the somber voice on the other end of the line told me that one of our players, Jayson Gwinn, had been killed in a car accident. What I found out is that Jayson, who was 20 years old and a promising defensive end, was returning home from hosting a recruit, and his car collided with the car of another Ohio State student at the corner of Olentangy River Road and Lane Avenue in Columbus. The accident occurred less than a mile from Ohio Stadium. To this day, no one knows who was at fault in this accident. One thing is for certain, Jayson Gwinn died at the scene.

Jayson was born into a remarkable, tight-knit family in Columbus. He played prep football at Brookhaven High School and was a highly touted recruit, earning All-Ohio and All-America honors. Jayson was also a remarkable individual. He worked hard and always reached his potential in the classroom and on the football field. He also was well-spoken and well-liked by everyone who met him. For me the loss was personal because I got to know the Gwinn family quite well during the recruiting process and then during his playing days. The entire family exuded love and compassion, and they were gracious and very spiritual. I had a special interest in Jayson because I was his position coach at Ohio State.

If the circumstances surrounding Jayson's death seem tragic, knowing the whole story makes it even more heart wrenching, and reinforces the notion that life is truly unfair at times. Jayson had just earned a starting position for the Buckeyes that year. In fact, he registered five tackles for a loss, two quarterback sacks, and was named Big Ten Defensive Player of the Week versus Indiana, whom we beat 23–17 just 29 days before his death. Jayson, like so many others that are taken so young, was only beginning to see what the future held for him. (Incidentally, Jayson's five tackles for loss remains a Buckeye Football record, tied with linebacker Andy Katzenmoyer, who also recorded five tackles for loss versus Arizona State in 1996.)

Though it is one of the saddest experiences in my life, Jayson's death also produced one of my most humbling experiences when his family asked me to perform the eulogy at his memorial service. It still chokes me up when I contemplate that day, when literally hundreds of people filed by the casket on display at Mershon Auditorium on the Ohio State campus. The day's events were captured and broadcasted by the media, which came from across the state to record the event. I had never eulogized someone before and was extremely nervous that I wouldn't do a good job. When I began to speak, however, the words seemed to flow as if they had a life of their own; maybe I was getting some unseen help? The truth is that Jayson was such a positive person that he, even in death, continued touching all of our lives. I had the opportunity to express what everyone in that auditorium was thinking . . . that we're here to celebrate the life of this special person. Jayson's legacy remains with the entire Ohio State Football family to this day, as well as the entire Columbus community. Brookhaven High School awards an annual academic scholarship in Jayson's name, and an annual youth football game—called the Jayson Gwinn Bowl—has been played since 2003. Compounding the influence of this young man is the fact that his younger brother, Anthony, played defensive back for the Buckeyes in the late 1990s. To this day, I consider the Gwinn family dear friends.

Both these stories exemplify the fact that the art of recruiting goes way beyond athletic performance and raw statistics. My relationship with the Gwinn family demonstrates the importance of building relationships with the families of recruits. The job of a good recruiter is to find out first and foremost who in the life of the recruit is helping them make their decision. Most of the time that individual is the recruit's parent, parents or guardian. Sometimes, however, it's a sibling, another relative or high school coach (not always football), teacher or principal. Sometimes it's the school counselor, or a family friend, or a church pastor. Successful recruiting involves asking the right questions of the right people. As a coach, you cannot allow your ego to get in the way of doing the job the right way. You must be a good conversationalist, but an even better listener. The more questions you ask, the more you understand the recruit as an individual, as well as the person he trusts to help him. You cannot take anything for granted, as the most ordinary detail about the university or the community may mean the difference between landing a recruit and playing against him on Saturdays. For example, a key reason one recruit whose story will be told later ultimately chose Ohio State is because Columbus, Ohio, has a large, respected, and socially and politically active Arab population.

The explosive use of the Internet since 1990 has had the greatest impact on college recruiting of any other outside influence to date. That is primarily because it forces coaches to make final decisions on prospects increasingly earlier each year. This is not a positive advancement. Today, coaches are expected to bring quality athletes, quality students and quality individuals to their institutions. If they do not do so, and mistakes are made or, worse yet, NCAA rules are broken, their reputations as coaches and individuals are in jeopardy. Statistics, profiles and accomplishments of high school athletes can be put on the Internet by anyone. Many times, these facts are not accurate and the college recruiter must do immediate research to determine the validity of the information. There is also the ever-present threat that the next so-called "great player" may commit somewhere else if you, as a college coach, do not make a scholarship offer. It's an intense, high-pressure process that can take its toll physically and emotionally for coaches.

The NCAA has not helped matters and has in many ways hurt the recruiting process. The NCAA has limited the college coach in the number of evaluations that can be performed (once in the fall and twice in May each year), number of phone calls and number of personal contacts with the recruit, his family and high school coach. Many times, coaches are forced to make intelligent decisions about recruits before they have completed their research. Sometimes coaches roll the dice and hope for the best.

There was once a time when a college coach could watch a prospect play several games his senior year and get into the high school several times to talk with coaches, teachers and counselors. A few years ago, the assistant coaches at Ohio State would leave after the team meal on Friday nights to go watch high school games. A skeleton crew of coaches would stay behind to take the college players back to the hotel where they were staying prior to Saturday's game. Coaches going to high school games would either drive or take a chartered plane, depending on the distance of the game. The Ohio State alumni who helped organize the flights were known as the "Buckeye Air Force." They would either pilot the airplanes themselves or make arrangements for such services to the coaches. In turn, the university would give them a gift-in-kind toward home game tickets and preferred seating.

None of these activities are permitted under current NCAA rules. As a college coach you are allowed to view a prospect in person one time his senior year and you hope he has a good game, otherwise he may vanish from your radar screen and a potential scholarship. This is why, when you decide to "roll them bones" on a particular recruit, you better hope it's the right decision for you and the recruit.

Conley's Recruiting Commandments

III. Don't make false promises.

Promise only those things you or the university can deliver. If you know you can't do it, or the progam or university can't deliver it, don't say it.

When I recruited tight end Ben Hartsock out of Unioto High School, a small rural district near the city of Chillicothe in southern Ohio, I only promised him a chance to compete. Ben was just happy to be a Buckeye, but with his skills and competitive spirit, he couldn't be kept off the field. He ended up being a key leader on the 2002 national championship team. He was an outstanding blocker and had very sure hands. He was so good that he's now playing for the Indianapolis Colts.

THE OHIO STATE UNIVERSITY BATTLING BUCKEYES

I was a senior in 1971 the year this team photo was taken.
That's me, No. 64, next to Coach Woody Hayes.

Nobody Did It Better Than Woody

I was stunned and a bit embarrassed when national recruiting guru Tom Lemming made this statement in November 2000 on ESPN's Web site: ". . . [Bill Conley] is the best recruiter since Woody Hayes." To be compared with Woody in any way, shape or form is a great compliment to anyone who bleeds Scarlet and Gray like me. As much as the quote humbled me, it also made me feel good that the long hours and many years of recruiting players to Ohio State was noticed by someone of Lemming's stature in the recruiting world. Even though Tom lives in Chicago, he is probably the most widely recognized recruiting authority in the business. He is largely responsible for choosing the *USA Today* All-America Team, as well as the U.S. Army All-American squad that plays in San Antonio, Texas, each January.

When it comes to recruiting, especially the art of "landing a key player," nobody did it better than Woody Hayes. He was the creator and master of the elements I call the Commandments of Recruiting. Woody left no stone unturned when it came to sifting through and understanding any and all details about a recruit's life. He was unmatched at the art of recruiting parents as well as the athlete. To be fair, during Woody's era most players came from two-parent homes, which made it easier to determine which parent was the primary decision maker of the family. The rules governing recruiting also were different during his career. There were many times that Woody would not hesitate to make an impromptu visit to a recruit's family, even if the recruit was not home. Don't think for a minute it was an accident that Woody just happened to stop by a barber shop owned by Rex Kern's father to get a trim, or shopped at a grocery story owned by the parents of Randy Gradishar. Woody honestly believed that if you recruited the parents hard enough, the player would follow the wishes of mom or dad. More times than not he was right, and I believe his record of success supports this contention.

Though Woody worked a recruit's family, he was just as strong or stronger at recruiting the individual athlete. He would never make false promises, but each player Woody zeroed in on was made to feel special. That was just his way. He would show up unexpectedly almost anywhere a recruit may be, whether it was at practices, a big game, or an unrelated sporting or social event at school. For a man who usually worked 18-hour days, he would somehow find time to personally recruit players. I know many head coaches cannot make this claim today and rely on their assistants to get the job of recruiting done. I believe this is a critical mistake.

A perfect example of Woody's persistence was at the state high school track meet in Columbus in 1977, where the late Todd Bell of Middletown was competing in the long jump at Ohio Stadium. Woody arrived at the meet in time to see Todd break Jessie Owens' long jump record. Was Woody really interested in track? Maybe. But Woody knew he had to attend that event and connect with this athlete on a personal level because every major college in the country wanted Todd Bell. This simple act of showing up at the right place at the right time usually paid huge dividends for Ohio State. In this particular case, it helped the Buckeye's land a great athlete. On signing day later that spring, legendary Michigan head coach Bo Schembechler arrived at Middletown High School early with the intentions of signing Bell to play for the Wolverines. At that time, coaches could be off campus with a recruit on the day of signing, as many highly recruited players wouldn't announce their college choice until that morning. Bo wanted desperately to beat Woody to the punch, but as Bo stood in the principal's office waiting for Todd to arrive, he happened to glance out the window to see Todd and Woody walking up the sidewalk together. I was told that Bo quietly uttered a colorful metaphor and left the building via a back door, knowing Woody had won this battle. Todd would go on to become a two-time All-Big Ten player and a standout with the Chicago Bears. Woody always took pride in the belief that no one could "out work" him, and in the case of Todd Bell it proved to be true.

Woody wasn't bashful about letting high school coaches know when the Buckeyes wanted one of their players. He was so well-respected and so well-feared by the coaches in the state that they willingly or sometimes unwillingly became extra recruiters for the program. You see, the last thing any high school coach in Ohio wanted was to be on the bad side of Woody Hayes. In fact, a majority of high school coaches strongly encouraged their players to continue their careers at Ohio State if they had a choice. Most of them did not want Woody to have the perception that they allowed a top-notch recruit go to a competing school, especially Michigan.

Part of the reason Woody was so well-respected by Ohio high school coaches, principals and superintendents was that they considered him to be "one of them." Woody had worked his way up through the ranks, beginning his career as a teacher and coach at Mingo Junction and New Philadelphia high schools in Ohio before moving to the college ranks. An English and history major, he always stressed the importance of academics. In fact, Woody was almost as widely respected for his knowledge of military history as he was his coaching skills.

Woody's influence transcended the borders of Ohio. During my first year recruiting in South Florida, I stopped by Santaluces High School near West Palm Beach. The principal of the school was so excited that a coach from Ohio State had stopped by to evaluate two of their football players that he wouldn't let me see the football coach until he could speak with me. I spent over an hour in his office before getting on with the task at hand. The principal wasn't being rude, but he had to tell me about the time Woody visited the school many years before on a recruiting trip. During the visit, Woody insisted on visiting a senior history class. Well, it seems that within minutes, the history teacher turned the class over to Woody, who then spent the next three periods teaching history to high school students in

Florida. The principal went on to explain how other students, teachers and administrators flocked to the room to watch Woody share his knowledge—and I'm sure his opinions—of world history. I'm pretty sure no one argued the facts or disagreed with his contentions. This story didn't shock me in the least, as it won't for anyone who knew and understood that Woody Hayes was an educator first and foremost, and never passed up an opportunity to teach, whether it was in the classroom or on the football field. Woody probably never returned to Santaluces, but the impression he made on that particular day had staying power, and the bridge he built made my job easier many years later.

A good recruiter asks the right questions. I believe good questions come from having a sincere interest in people, and showing a sincere interest in people creates a bond of trust that is not easily broken. These are traits that helped me be successful as a recruiter, traits I honed listening, watching and learning from Woody Hayes. It usually didn't take Woody long to figure out what made a recruit tick and what bells to push to get a commitment. If he didn't, he would tell one of his assistant coaches to ask a particular question. Woody used this technique to determine if a recruit was merely saying things they thought the head coach would want to hear. This way, Woody could determine the sincerity, temperament and personality traits of a recruit.

Back in the days when recruits could stay at the head coach's house during official visits, Woody's wife, Anne, would regularly have recruits butter the toast for breakfast at their Cardiff Avenue home in Upper Arlington, an affluent suburb of

Columbus. As in all things involving Woody, there was a specific game plan already sketched out for this activity. Anne would be prepared with a number of questions to ask during polite, relaxed conversation when the coach wasn't in the room. After a recruit left, Anne would give Woody a comprehensive report on what they said, including her perceptions about what she believed they meant by what they said. I know for a fact that if a recruit could not pass the "Anne Test," they usually didn't get much further in the process, and probably did not play for Ohio State.

I mentioned it before, but another primary reason Woody Hayes was an outstanding recruiter was that he truly and geniunely cared about people. There was nothing false about Woody, and most people either loved him or hated him. I've met very few people who do not have a firm opinion of the coach. Anyone who ever played for him understood that it was "all business" when they went on the field. Woody demanded perfection and used whatever methods he believed necessary to get the attention of his players. If that meant ripping up his hat, breaking a watch, giving a player a jab, or making up a story that spies from Michigan were on campus, so be it. Although he didn't hold the necessary academic degrees, Woody was a natural motivator and sports psychologist, who seemed to possess a bottomless arsenal of tactics.

I will never forget a trip to Michigan during my playing days in 1971. Traveling north on U.S. Route 23 toward Ann Arbor, Woody suddenly ordered the bus driver to pull over just a few miles across the Michigan state line. If the maneuver in heavy traffic wasn't shocking enough, what came next left all of us stunned. Woody stood at the front of the bus, and for the next 15 minutes gave us a lecture on the "Fall of the Roman Empire." Why? Well, it seems that before we left Columbus, Woody picked up a copy of *The Lantern,* the Ohio State student newspaper. In an article discussing the game we were about to play, the sports editor picked Michigan to win. Woody must have stewed on this for most of the trip before stopping the buses. Once he finished his lecture about how the Roman Empire was torn apart from within, the always demonstrative Woody Hayes opened the door of the bus, crumpled up the copy of the newspaper and threw it outside. What he didn't realize was that assistant coach John Mummey was standing at the door. You see, Mummey was riding in a second bus used to transport the team, and had walked forward to determine just why the buses had stopped. Well, the copy of *The Lantern* struck Coach Mummey square in the face. Not a word was said as Woody, who probably didn't realize what had just happened, ordered the bus driver to close the doors and get moving. Still stunned, Mummey watched as the bus began to pull back on the highway, and then sprinted to return to his bus so it could continue the trip. Now, the Roman Empire analogy was inspirational, and the Coach Mummey incident was hysterical, but don't think for a moment that any of us laughed.

Besides Woody's bus lecture, this game is also infamous as one where Woody threw one of his classic sideline tirades. With time running down and Michigan winning, Buckeye quarterback Don Lamka attempted to orchestrate a late-game comeback. Guiding the Buckeyes down the field, he threw a pass to receiver Dick Wakefield that was intercepted by Michigan defensive back Thom Darden. To most Buckeye fans in the stadium and watching at home on television, it appeared as if

Darden interfered with Wakefield, but the referees never called a penalty. Woody went berserk, breaking sideline markers and screaming profanities at the refs. He even stormed onto the field, getting to mid-field before being pulled back to the sidelines by several players. The outburst cost the Buckeyes 30 yards in penalties, and we would lose the hard-fought game, 10–7. When asked about the incident after the game, Michigan coach Bo Schembechler said he believed that Woody knew exactly what he was doing, and that that incident would be used to motivate the Buckeyes for the following year's contest. You know, Bo was probably correct in his assessment, as the Buckeyes won the 1972 contest in Columbus, 14–11.

As tough as Woody was on us, he never allowed anyone else to make a negative comment about his "boys." Whether it meant helping players be admitted to graduate school, tutoring those having difficulty in class, or making a job recommendation, Woody was always the first one to step up to support one of his players. This is why he remains such an enigma in the minds of many people. But he is only that way for those who didn't know him. Again, Woody Hayes just did not know how to fake any part of his personality, the good parts or the bad parts. He was what he was, and anything he portrayed was genuine.

Woody's concern for others went beyond the team. He was the first coach to take players to Children's Hospital to visit with children who were battling a variety of serious and often deadly illnesses. He traveled throughout Ohio making speech after speech in support of school districts trying to pass tax levies, and wouldn't take a single penny to do so. As a matter of fact, the only time I know of Woody accepting money for a speaking engagement was the time a former equipment manager Phil Bennett had been diagnosed with terminal cancer. Woody secretly gave the money to Bennett's family to help cover mounting medical costs.

Woody Hayes loved The Ohio State University. This was best demonstrated during the student demonstrations and riots that plagued college campuses over the Vietnam War in the spring of 1970, and which came to a head on May 4 when four students were shot and killed by Ohio National Guardsmen at Kent State University in Kent, Ohio. Many universities chose to close their doors, and one person who was largely responsible for keeping Ohio State open was Woody Hayes. Just as Ohio State students—who were stirred up by non-student, anti-war agitators—were preparing to riot that day, Woody (who was flanked by several of his players) marched to the middle of campus, a place called the Oval, and gave one of his "God and Country" speeches. The emotion and conviction of his words touched everyone within earshot, and while it did not stop student protests, I truly believe it prevented a Kent State-like incident from happening here. I also believe it helped the university remain open to complete the spring quarter.

Unfortunately, the university he loved so much, and for which he put himself at risk would fire him less than a decade later following the now infamous Gator Bowl incident. Even so, Woody never showed anomosity toward the university and remained a Buckeye and Ohio State supporter until his death in 1987. This fact among others shows the depth of character he possessed.

Woody loved the United States of America. He had served in the U.S. Navy during World War II, and always felt an obligation to support our country's troops. During the Vietnam War, he would travel to that country in the off-season armed with his 16–millimeter projector and game films. In the evenings, he would have the soldiers hang a bedsheet outside the barracks and show films, providing colorful commentary. He often made the trip with entertainer Bob Hope, a Cleveland native who was a longtime friend and Buckeye fan. As a matter of fact, Woody Hayes, Bob Hope and former world-champion boxer James "Buster" Douglas are the only non-band members to "dot the i" in the famous script "Ohio" during halftime of a football game at Ohio Stadium.

As loyal as Woody was to his country, even U.S. presidents had to wait for him from time to time. Following a 20–9 victory over Michigan in 1970, equipment manager John Bozick broke into the middle of Woody's victory speech to say that "the president is on the phone."

"What president?" Woody inquired in a scolding tone.

"President Nixon. The president of the United States," Bozick replied.

Without hesitation, Woody blurted out, "Tell him to wait. The team comes first."

Needless to say, a roar erupted from the players that shook the locker room. Didn't I say that the "Old Man" had a way of making his players feel special?

A similar scenario repeated itself in 1974, following another Buckeye victory over Michigan. This time, it was President Gerald Ford, a Michigan native, who had to wait until Woody was done talking to his boys.

Recruiter, educator, humanitarian and statesman are all words that can be used to describe the late, great Woody Hayes. His detractors would include a litany of profanities and barbs to this list. The bottom line with Woody, however, was that he was no phony; he was real, and he was absolute. Most importantly, he was a coach. He was our coach. Woody Hayes was born on Valentine's Day, but very few players knew this fact as he never told them for fear they would believe he was "a softie."

So, for Tom Lemming to compare me with Woody was indeed an honor. I like to believe the skills I have as a teacher, coach and recruiter were inspired and instilled by him. Ultimately, however, I (or anyone else for that matter) could never be another Woody Hayes, and I wouldn't want to be. He wouldn't want me to be someone other than myself, as he would want me to learn from both the positive and negative aspects of his personality and find my own way. I believe that's what I did during my tenure at Ohio State and continue striving to do today.

Conley's Recruiting Commandments

IV. Ask the right questions.

Listening is the key to knowing what questions to ask of recruits and/or the primary decision maker to better sell your program.

While recruiting cornerback Ashton Youboty from Klein, Texas, I needed to find out as soon as possible if he would consider leaving Texas to go to college. I discovered that he had moved to Texas from Philadelphia in the eighth grade. A native of Liberia, Ashton wanted a Big Ten education, so his decision came down to Ohio State and Penn State. I believe we outworked and outwitted the Nittany Lion staff, and Ashton ultimately decided to major in finance at The Ohio State University. He was a junior on the 2005 Buckeye football team.

CHRIS SPIELMAN   OHIO STATE

Chris Spielman during
his time as a Buckeye
(above).

Cris Carter (left) as a
Middletown Middie.

Earle, Chris and Cris

I've always admired Earle Bruce as a football coach and as an individual, and I feel fortunate to be able to consider him a dear friend. The first time I met Earle was when he was an assistant coach to Woody Hayes and I was one of 100 walk-ons trying to make the Ohio State team in 1968. Fortunately for me, he was my position coach and had the biggest influence on Woody Hayes offering me a scholarship during my playing days. Earle was an excellent technician of the game and he took pride in the fact that his players were sound in executing the fundamentals of their position. When you played for Earle, there was no time for nonsense. Woody demanded great concentration and effort on the field and Earle was no different. He reflected the same intensity on the field as Woody, and when he was named head football coach at Ohio State after Woody, the similarities between their styles were striking.

Earle gave me the chance to break into college football coaching in the summer of 1984, and for that I will always be grateful and in his debt. Going from high school coaching to a major college program like Ohio State wasn't easy. I found the college game to be much more complicated and detailed than high school football, from a coaching perspective. That aspect of the profession takes care of itself, however, as you become more experienced. The biggest transition is the time commitment necessary to be successful at the college level. Every aspect of the game takes longer to perfect and requires greater effort. Practices are more intense, and you spend more time reviewing and breaking down film and in meetings preparing for games. Add the responsibility of recruiting and it's easy to understand why the coaching profession causes family stress. The sacrifices, which are sometimes severe, are countered by the adrenaline rush football coaches get from helping players reach their potential. Maybe this is why so few people are cut out to do it. And maybe this is why for those who survive there's nothing like it.

The opportunity given me by Earle Bruce permitted me to follow the path of one great athlete beyond the high school level, and get acquainted with another who would forever change the standard by which I compare athletes. The latter is Chris Spielman, and the former is Cris Carter. The following will examine the careers and my involvement with both these special football players.

Chris Spielman: Defining Desire and Intensity

Joining Earle Bruce's coaching staff introduced me to one of the most intense and dedicated athletes I believe I will ever know. That athlete is none other than Chris Spielman.

I did not recruit Chris Spielman to play for Ohio State. Actually, we both arrived at the university the summer of 1984. He was a celebrated freshman from the high school–football factory town of Massillon, Ohio—the kid who got his face on a box of Wheaties—and I was a new assistant coach. I got to know Chris quite well, however, as Coach Bruce assigned me to coach linebackers. To me, Chris is the archetype of desire, determination and intrinsic motivation. I still use traits he exhibited as a baseline measurement in assessing Division I college football or professional football recruits today.

Having stated that, I'll never forget the first time I met Chris in the hallway at the Woody Hayes Athletic Center. It was during freshmen check-in prior to the start of summer practices. Chris asked me directions to the equipment room, and I told him to check in with our equipment manager to get his assignment. You see, I thought this comparatively small, lean, flat-footed kid was one of our new student managers. I still didn't believe him when he said, "No, I'm supposed to get my gear and head to the locker room. I'm a new freshman; my name is Chris Spielman."

"This is the much-heralded Chris Spielman I heard so much about?" I thought to myself. "He's not big enough to survive the rigors of Division I football, especially at Ohio State."

I know what you're thinking, but at that time one of our starting linebackers was Thomas "Pepper" Johnson, who at 6 feet 5 inches and 250 pounds was a prototypical Division I linebacker. Pepper also was a great football player and set the standard of performance on our defense. He was a two-time co-captain and defensive MVP for the Buckeyes, and won All-America honors as a senior in 1985. Pepper went on to enjoy a 13-year NFL career, where he was elected to play in two Pro Bowls, and won two Super Bowl titles (1986 and 1990) as a member of the New York Giants. In 1999, Pepper was named to the Buckeye "All-Century" team, and in 2001 he was inducted into the Ohio State Athletics Hall of Fame. Need I say more?

So you can't blame me for having initial doubts when I met this kid who was barely 6 feet tall and weighed just 200 pounds. Don't worry, Chris would quickly make me a fervent disciple of the adage: "It's not the size of the dog in the fight, but the size of the fight in the dog that counts."

Let me share a story I learned from Chris' childhood that truly explains the inner fire that fueled this young man to the athletic heights he achieved. During one family outing in his youth, Chris' parents took him to visit the Pro Football Hall of Fame in Canton, Ohio, which is just down the highway from Massillon. At that time, he was a promising youth football player, so the men enshrined there and the deeds they performed on the gridiron enthralled and inspired him. At the end of the tour, Chris' parents, Sonny and Nancy, told him he could visit the gift shop and pick out one item. Now, you can only imagine the excitement that must have been boiling inside of him. What merchandise, what piece of memorabilia would he choose to buy to honor this special day? Would it be a T-shirt? No. Would he select a pennant, a video or a miniature bust of his favorite player? No. How about something from his favorite team, the Cleveland Browns? No, again. What Chris chose that fateful day was a 50-cent bumper sticker, which simply read: NFL. It's all he wanted, and he went home and stuck it on the ceiling above his bed. He did that so the bumper sticker was the first thing he saw when he woke up and the last thing he saw before falling to sleep. That bumper sticker summed up what this young man was about to dedicate the prime years of his life achieving, and he would not be denied.

That story speaks volumes about this special athlete. But there's more. I knew my first impressions of Chris were wrong after we began summer practices. He possessed a level of intensity and desire that couldn't be faked. He made a routine out of staying late after practices by himself to either run, lift or perform drills that would enhance his linebacker skills. The first time I saw this he was going back and forth along a spring-backed board we called the shiver board, which we used to strengthen players' wrists, hands and forearms. This is essential for defenders—especially defensive linemen and linebackers—to keep blockers away from your body. Chris was doing this long after the rest of the team had left the practice field.

I approached Chris, who was sweating profusely as he worked to increase the speed of his repetitions, saying, "You know practice is over, don't you? Let's get to the training table."

"I will, Coach," he panted. "I just need to do more reps. I've got to get better if we're going to beat Michigan."

Now that's what you want to hear when you're coaching at Ohio State!

I thought this was a one-time thing, a way for a cocksure freshman to make additional brownie points with the coaching staff. But this became Chris' routine throughout his college and professional football careers. He was also the first player in the weight room for conditioning and put more time in with film than any other player I've had the pleasure of coaching.

A brief look at Chris' prep school, college and professional statistics and awards shows how individual desire and determination can sometimes overshadow raw physical talent, or lack thereof. An All-American at Washington High School near Massillon, Chris was named the top prep linebacker in the nation by

Parade magazine his senior year. (As a sidebar, I find it interesting that most people don't know that the *Wheaties* thing was really a promotional contest created by the cereal maker. The community that sent in the most proof of purchase seals got to select a local athlete to put on the box. Yes, the winner was Massillon.) The only promotion Chris required at Ohio State was his on-field performance each and every Saturday. Chris earned a starting spot his freshman year, and eventually became a two-time All-America and a three-time All-Big Ten selection. By his senior year, he had grown to 6 feet 1 inch and bulked up to more than 230 pounds.

A devastating hitter, Chris remains Ohio State's all-time leader in solo tackles in a season (105 in 1986), and most solo tackles in a career (283 between 1984 and 1987). He tied Tom Cousineau's record for most tackles in a game, with 29 in 1986 versus Michigan and is among the university's all-time leading tacklers overall with 546.

In addition to All-America honors his junior and senior years (1986–87), Chris won the Lombardi Award his senior year. The Lombardi Award is given annually to the nation's best linebacker, and it's an honor he well-deserved.

Despite his performance, statistics and awards, many pro scouts questioned whether Chris could play in the NFL because of his size and speed. The one element some scouts ignored was the size of his heart and depth of desire.

The Detroit Lions selected Chris with the first pick of the second round of 1988 draft. During the next eight seasons, he earned Pro Bowl honors four times. He established a Lions' record by leading the team in tackles for eight straight seasons. Chris also never missed a game during his time with the Lions.

In his first nine years as a pro, Chris played in 114 consecutive games. (It's ironic that a few years later, then Cincinnati Bengals head coach Sam Wyche told me they had made a mistake in passing up Chris in the first round, and instead took a player who was bigger and faster, but did not make it in the NFL.)

Chris played two years with the Buffalo Bills before joining the Cleveland Browns after the 1998 season. When his wife, Stephanie, was diagnosed with breast cancer in 1999, Chris took a year off to be at home with her and their children. He made national headlines when he shaved his head (to match his wife's hair loss during chemotherapy) to help his children understand and not be afraid of what their mother was going through. Chris returned to the Browns the following year, only to suffer a career-ending neck injury.

Since retiring from football, Chris has been a regular voice on a Columbus sports radio station and has covered college football for ESPN. In 2003, he became general manager of the Columbus Destroyers of the Arena Football League, a move that once again teamed him up with Earle Bruce, who was head coach. In 2004, Chris took over as head coach in addition to his duties as general manger of the Destroyers, and he would coach the team during the 2005 campaign.

What Chris' career and life exemplify are the fortitude of his personality and the passion he puts into every endeavor. This is why he—or rather the traits he personifies—are the standard I've used to measure recruits.

Cris Carter: Basketball Prodigy Becomes NFL Star

Few high school football coaches get an opportunity to play a part of an athlete's development beyond the twelfth grade. The fact that I got an opportunity to do just that with Cris Carter is one reason why he owns a special spot in my heart and my life. I met Cris in June 1982 after I was hired as head football coach at Middletown High School in Middletown, Ohio. At the time, Cris was a young man with much athletic potential who had the unsavory lot of being the younger brother of Middletown basketball legend Clarence "Butch" Carter. Butch Carter was an Ohio Player of the Year and led the Middletown Middies his senior year to the state tournament finals. Butch Carter was then a standout player and eventual co-captain of the Indiana Hoosiers in the early 1970s, where he was famous for shooting the winning basket in an NIT title game. Butch was a second-round draft pick of the Los Angeles Lakers in the late 1970s and played six seasons in the NBA before leaving to become a basketball coach. During a short stint as the Middies head coach between 1986 and 1988, he earned Ohio Coach of the Year honors—the only person to win both top player and top coach honors in Ohio. Butch Carter left the Middies to become an assistant coach at the University of Dayton, and then an assistant coach with the Milwaukee Bucks in the NBA. Butch Carter was head coach of the Toronto Raptors at the time this book was written.

Now you can see why those close to Cris believed he might want to follow in his brother's footsteps and focus on basketball, and for a while Cris considered doing just that. After the first day of early summer speed and agility camp at Middletown High School, however, I honestly wondered how he ever got downfield without falling down. By day five of the camp, Cris was showing greater balance and agility than most of the other athletes, but he was still quite a distance from the college and NFL star he would become. I'll discuss this in greater depth along with a feat of pure athleticism that would forever change my mind about Cris. First, allow me to share how the fates put me in this spot at this particular time, and how this experience would alter my professional life.

I resigned as head football coach at Groveport High School after three seasons to replace Jack Gordon, who was retiring after 18 seasons as head coach at Middletown High School. Don't get me wrong, I was very happy coaching at Groveport, and we were beginning to build a successful program. It's just that the Middletown job was considered one of a few "holy grail" coaching positions in Ohio, so to speak. Why? Here was a program that experienced just six losing seasons in the 60 prior to my arrival. Yes, you read that correctly . . . six! Gordon amassed a 114–60–1 career record, but he wasn't the only Middletown coach to hold a 65 percent or greater win rate. Before Gordon, there was the legendary Glenn "Tiger" Ellison, the father of the modern day "run and shoot" offense, and a man who was one my chief influences at Ohio State, where he was my freshman coach. A Middletown alumnus, member of its Athletic Hall of Fame, and the namesake of its football stadium, Ellison recorded a 124–46–9 career record (.693 percent win rate) between 1945 and 1962. The Middletown tradition superceded Ellison, who replaced Elmo Lingrel. Between 1923 and 1944, Lingrel amassed a record of 149–32–19 (or .745 percent). Legendary coaches, however, are only as good as their assistants and their players, and Middletown had a reputation for producing generations of good football players. This industrial community in western Ohio eats, breathes and lives the game of football. It's a passion, and that passion fuels expectations for winning like no community I've encountered in my prep coaching experience. (Some would argue that passion is endemic throughout Ohio, and is equal to what you'd find in other winning programs in cities such as Massillon, Cleveland, Cincinnati, Columbus, Canton, Dayton, Toledo and Youngstown.) From my experience, it is not a stretch to say the passion the Middletown community had for the Middies is akin to the passion Ohio State fans have for the Buckeyes, just on a smaller scale.

As was my custom after taking over any new program, I spoke with each returning player individually so I could get to know him and vice versa. On the day I was scheduled to speak with Cris, the coaching staff just happened to be moving weight-lifting equipment from one school building to another. Because I had several players on hand, I asked them if they would mind helping to make the job easier and go faster. At the loading dock, Cris stood on the driveway next to the truck as the coaches prepared to load a Universal gym. Seeing that they could use some assistance, I asked Cris to get up on the loading dock to help. What happened next is something I can only describe as one of those "holy shit moments," or those moments when you really cannot believe what you see happening. Instead of walking up steps at the side of the loading dock to get where he was needed, Cris simply bent his knees and, from a flat-footed stance, jumped the three-foot, vertical distance from the driveway to the floor of the loading dock platform with ease. I still remember looking at a wide-eyed, dropped-jawed expression on the face of our offensive line coach, Brian "Dawg" Warning, when I said: "Dawg, this is no ordinary human being." All Dawg could do is nod, and we went about our business. That incident would replay over and over in my head each time I saw Cris perform one of his patented flying, twisting, seemingly impossible receptions as a high school, college and then professional football player. Cris wasn't an ordinary human being.

During my conversation with Cris later that day, he mentioned that he was in a quandary about whether to play football his junior year or quit to focus on basketball. To my chagrin, it appeared as if his basketball pedigree was winning some internal battle for his athletic soul. I didn't immediately respond to his comment; actually, I couldn't speak until my heart returned from my feet where it had figuratively dropped. Regaining my composure, I told Cris that I admired him for trying to set personal goals. I told him he should consider playing both sports his junior year before making a decision to focus on one, and to leave his options open. I also told him that if after his junior year he wanted to focus on basketball, I would support that decision and help him in any way possible to play in college. I was having yet another "holy shit moment" and it involved the same person on the same day. Fortunately for the modern football world, Cris continued with the sport two more seasons. As a testament to the athletic talent this young man possessed, he would go on to earn All-Ohio honors in both football and basketball as a senior.

It is no hyperbole for me to state that Cris Carter was the best high school athlete I ever had the privilege of coaching. He could have been a starter for us at quarterback (he could throw a football 60 yards on a rope), or safety (he was the hardest hitter on the team). But the position he was born to play was wide receiver, and it is in that position where he was destined to leave an indelible mark. Cris was not the fastest player on the team (he ran a 4.6-second 40-yard dash in high school), but he was intelligent, ran flawless routes and had amazing leaping ability and sponge-like hands under pressure—all traits that would help him become an All-American at Ohio State and a Hall of Fame-caliber player for the Minnesota Vikings in the late 1980s and 1990s.

At that particular moment, however, the Buckeyes and the Vikings were not even on Cris' radar screen. He had to focus on his junior season. The team I inherited at Middletown had an agonizing 3–7 season the prior year. We rebounded in 1982 to post a 6–4 record. Cris earned All-Conference and second-team All-Ohio honors. Needless to say, we were excited about the next season, when Cris and a host of talented players would return as seniors.

At 6 feet 3 inches and 195 pounds, Cris was a preseason All-America selection in 1983. Like a thorn in your shoe, the most irritating question was whether he would play football or decide to quit to focus on basketball. Much to my relief, Cris decided to play football and applied himself in an off- and preseason fitness regimen. To say Cris was an intense player is an understatement. Cris approached each practice as if it were a game, and at times we had to tell him to take the intensity down a notch for fear he would hurt one of his teammates. A good example of Cris' intensity was seen in a pre-season scrimmage verses Cincinnati Moeller (another tradition-rich high school football program and once an Ohio juggernaut). Playing safety on defense, Cris pounced on a toss sweep play, coming up so hard and so fast that he knocked out the opposing ball carrier while making the tackle. That particular Moeller player probably had a headache for a couple days, but I'm sure he still tells the story today about his encounter with the great Cris Carter. Cris played a starring role on a 1983 Middies team that went 9–1 and outscored its opponents 358–115. Our only loss that season was to the eventual state champion Cincinnati Princeton, who beat us 23–22 on a field so flooded by torrential rains that a police helicopter was used to help dry it prior to kickoff. Both teams were undefeated entering the game, which featured not only the two fastest teams in the state, but also 11 eventual Division I college players, including Cris.

Throughout his senior season, Cris was a playmaker and our "go to" guy. In a game against Cincinnati Withrow, which we won 48–0, Cris had four blocked punts, four touchdown receptions and a punt return for a touchdown. Even though that is impressive in itself, one play at the end of our fourth game against Newark truly exemplified Cris' game intelligence and raw athletic ability. With fewer than three minutes remaining in the game and our lead cut to four points, we were facing fourth down and long with the ball on our own five-yard line, which meant we would be punting from our own end zone. To be safe, I instructed quarterback Al Milton (also our punter) to kick the ball as far as he could and allow our defense to protect the lead. I didn't know it until after the play that, when the team huddled, Cris reminded Al that if the defense left him uncovered (we split him out wide to get downfield to cover the punt), he would be wide open on the outside. After all, who would be crazy enough to pass the ball this deep on their end of the field, and risk destroying an undefeated season and a possible state playoff berth? Well, when Cris lined up and saw that he was uncovered, he shot Al a pre-designed hand signal calling for the fake, and for Al to throw him the ball. I realized too late what was happening, and the ball was already snapped before I could call timeout. The next thing I saw was Al heaving the ball downfield and Cris sprinting up the sideline. Not only was our coaching staff caught off guard—you should have heard the profanity pounding in my headset—but so was Newark. After what seemed like an eternity, the ball fell into Cris' hands at the 35-yard line and he sprinted down the field before being tackled at Newark's 30-yard line, giving us a first and 10 and securing the victory. My assistant coaches in the press box overheard the announcer say, "it was the greatest coaching call he had ever seen." Little did the announcer know that my heart stopped when the ball was lofted and didn't start beating again until the play was over. After the game, a still-befuddled Newark head coach Bill Biggers came up to shake my hand, asking, "What if that pass was incomplete, Coach?" All I could think of retorting was, "I'd be staying at your house tonight because I couldn't go back to Middletown."

Cris finished his senior season as one of the most highly coveted blue-chip recruits in America. Ohio State was one of a number of schools vying for Cris, including the dreaded Michigan Wolverines. Buckeye head coach Earle Bruce attended our pivotal game against Princeton and stayed long enough into the second half to see Cris go up for a pass between two defenders, snare the ball with one hand and bring it down for a touchdown. Middletown athletic director Ed "Skeeter" Payne shared with me later that, after that particular play, the Ohio State coach jumped up and kicked his chair back shouting, "I don't need to see any more . . . that kid needs to be a Buckeye!" Other schools in the mix included Notre Dame and the University of Southern California for football and Louisville for basketball.

Ultimately, it was Cris' height, or lack thereof in relation to basketball, that swayed his decision to pursue a scholarship to play football in college. Again, the world of football had a collective sigh of relief. I got an inkling of Cris' ultimate decision on the afternoon we visited Ohio State on our way to the Newark game. Because we had to go through Columbus, I thought it would be inspiring for the boys to visit the Horseshoe, and walk on the same field where many of their childhood heroes played. So we left Middletown two hours early and made a detour when we reached Columbus. I made arrangements for the boys to walk onto the field, and as they walked I could see Cris absorbing the experience, and it took me back to my playing days not so many years ago.

"You should stand here when the stands are full," I remarked to Cris and some other players. "And when the band comes out, all hell breaks loose."

Then, looking at Cris, I said, "Son, you do know you are good enough to play here, don't you?"

His grin said it all as he said, "I might just have to do that, Coach."

By the end of the 1984 recruiting season, the only schools remaining on Cris' radar were Notre Dame, USC and Ohio State. On the Monday morning after Cris visited South Bend, Jerry Faust, the former Cincinnati Moeller High School coach who was now head coach of the Fighting Irish, was waiting for me when I arrived at school. Jerry seemed very excited and was convinced that Cris was going to accept the scholarship offer to play at Notre Dame.

"I think we have ourselves a new player," the confident, raspy voiced Faust said, shaking my hand.

"Is that so?" I responded.

"I'm sure of it. I think Cris was impressed with our program and our school," he replied.

About that time, Cris walked in and I let him and Coach Faust use my office to have some privacy. They were only in the office for about 15 minutes when the coach emerged with a very distraught expression on his face. In a defeated tone, he informed me that Cris wasn't going to Notre Dame. We shook hands and he left to travel back to South Bend. Later, Cris told me that he liked the school and indeed respected the football program, but disliked South Bend and couldn't see himself living there.

Weather, of all things, played a big part in Cris' decision to eliminate USC. One of the USC assistant coaches was scheduled to come to Middletown to set up Cris' official visit. As fate would have it, a violent winter storm hit and the coach was unable to make the connection to Columbus from Chicago. Instead of waiting the storm out, he decided to return to Los Angeles, a move Cris interpreted as a lack of interest, so the Trojans were eliminated from consideration. (Years later that USC assistant would see Cris at the Rose Bowl and tell Cris he made a huge mistake by not waiting the storm out.)

By mid-January of his senior year, and to the satisfaction and thrill of most people in Middletown and many across Ohio, Cris decided to be a Buckeye. Being a former player, it was especially gratifying for me. I was looking forward to following his career in Columbus. Little did I know at that time that I would be changing venues as well, and would continue to watch his progress from the sidelines.

Cris would go on to become a star player at Ohio State, earning All-America honors in 1986 as a junior before leaving early for the NFL draft. When he left, Cris held the Ohio State record for receptions (168) and touchdown catches (27) and appeared in the Rose Bowl as a freshman. Cris was drafted by the Philadelphia Eagles in 1987 and joined the Minnesota Vikings in 1990. He caught an NFL record 122 passes in 1994 and repeated that total in 1995. Cris holds the most Viking records for pass receivers and is listed among the top 10 all-time receivers in NFL history. He was second-team all-NFL in 1995 and set a league record with two or more touchdowns in four straight games. He was the second player in NFL history to reach 1,000 career catches. Cris retired from the NFL in 2003 to pursue a career in broadcasting. He also owns and operates a sports performance and training center in Boca Raton, Florida, and a security company in Atlanta.

As for me, you know the story. Coach Bruce contacted me later that spring and asked me to join his staff. I truly intended to finish my high school teaching and coaching career at Middletown, as I was just that happy. But I would be a fool to turn down an opportunity to join the college ranks. I resigned myself to the fact that fate had other plans for me, and I officially joined the Ohio State Buckeyes as an assistant coach in the summer of 1984. I must point out that, as a high school coach, you get well-acquainted with most of the players on your team. At the college level—especially at the Division I level—you get close to those players in the positions for which you are responsible, but it's difficult to know every single player. Although Cris and I remain great friends today, I didn't play an intimate role in his development after high school. My immediate responsibility for the Buckeyes was with linebackers. Still, I always took great pride in the job my staff at Middletown and

I did getting Cris Carter ready for the next level. We were honest about what he'd experience, and how most of those playing against him were also high school stars in their own right. I believe it's the duty of a high school coach to be completely honest with all of his players, particularly as it pertains to their potential at the college level. As you will see, future Heisman Trophy winner Eddie George had some difficulties developing into the college game, and so did Cris.

I vividly remember Cris' first game in Ohio Stadium. He dropped a slant pass that hit him square in the hands. Being the great player that he was, he bounced back and set a reception record for a freshman that day. After the game, I went up to Cris in the locker room and laughingly asked how he could drop the very first pass thrown to him at Ohio State? He looked me in the eyes and said, "Coach Conley, there's more people out there than in the entire city of Middletown."

Cris would go on to make incredible receptions—such as the acrobatic sideline catch in the Citrus Bowl against Brigham Young, where he went vertical to snag the ball out of the air. Brigham Young coach Lavelle Edwards would even call it the greatest catch he had ever seen.

It's players such as Chris Spielman and Cris Carter that truly define greatness in an athlete. Both were natural talents that were developed and honed to their maximum levels through hard work and dedication. Both athletes loved to compete, thrived when competition was stronger and would not accept anything less than perfection of themselves and those around them. This is the definition of a champion.

Conley's Recruiting Commandments

V. Pick the right host.

During official visits match recruits with players of similar personality traits and/or ethnic and socio-economic backgrounds to make for a positive experience.

All-American place kicker Mike Nugent was as good a recruiting host as he was a player. When we had recruits with high academic goals, high football goals and great spiritual values, we put them with Mike. Mike was completely unselfish with his time and was a great proponent of Ohio State, and we landed nearly every recruit he was assigned. (Read more about Mike in chapter 9.)

Na'il Diggs (#32) wraps up a Michigan ball carrier in a 31–16 victory in 1998.

It's Competitive Out There

. . . So sometimes it doesn't hurt to be lucky

As competition for top recruits increases among major universities, the seemingly most insignificant point may mean the difference of landing a recruit or not. Two stories in particular, one recent and another from the mid-1990s, dramatize the point that sometimes fate, luck or both play their part in the recruiting process. In both cases, I can neither credit art nor science for a chain reaction of events that brought two new Buckeye players to Columbus.

Nader Abdallah: Getting Some Help from the President of the United States

It was late January 2004 and the third-floor room at the Airport Hilton near New Orleans was dark, so I pulled open the drapes to let some light in. Finally able to see, I glanced at my watch and realized I had 45 minutes to take a shower and relax for a moment before a 2 P.M. meeting with the father and eldest brother of a recruit I had been pursuing for nearly two months. The recruit was high school All-American defensive lineman Nader Abdallah from Archbishop Rummel High School in Metairie, Louisiana, a suburb of New Orleans.

Glancing up, something caught my eye that underscored a strange series of events I'll never forget. I saw Air Force One sitting on the runway no more than 400 yards from my hotel room. As I stood there staring at the airplane, an entourage of white New Orleans police cruisers and at least a half-dozen black, SUV limousines pulled up to it. I could see President George W. Bush as he climbed the steps, waved to a small crowd of people and stepped into Air Force One. Within minutes, several of the limos were flanking the aircraft as it taxied down the runway and lifted off.

Absorbed in my curiosity, I failed to notice that three other limos had pulled into the hotel parking lot, and were now stopping directly below my window. Several men who could only be Secret Service agents quickly exited the vehicles and looked as if they were staring in my direction.

"Oh, my God, they saw me watching and think I'm some kind of terrorist," I cringed to myself.

Now flushed and trembling, I quickly closed the drapes, sat down on the bed and tried to regain my composure. More of this story later . . .

I traveled to New Orleans to recruit Abdallah, who was a prep phenomenon at Archbishop Rummel High School. At 6 feet

3 inches and 295 pounds, he embodied the ideal Division I interior defensive lineman with his speed, quickness, good hands, power and game sense. In addition to his physical gifts, what made Nader even more unique is the fact that he would be the first player of Palestinian descent to play Division I college football. Additionally, he was not only an exceptional athlete, but also a dedicated and disciplined student, and well-mannered and well-spoken individual.

I learned about Nader in mid-December 2003 from respected recruiter and promoter Tom Lemming, who tapped Nader to play in the prestigious U.S. Army All-American Game in San Antonio, Texas. Ohio State doesn't recruit Louisiana on a regular basis, but we were poised to lose several outstanding senior defensive linemen, including Tim Anderson (All-Big Ten), Darrion Scott and Will Smith (All-America). I also thought it was wise to at least give this young man a look as you never know where you'll find the next Chris Spielman or Eddie George. (The only other player we recruited from Louisiana prior to Nader was running back Jonathon Wells, who came to Ohio State in 1998.)

A review of game film affirmed the talent Nader possessed on the football field. One game in particular, versus Shreveport Evangel in the Louisiana state playoffs stands out in my mind. The quarterback for Shreveport was senior Jonathon Booty, also a nationally coveted recruit. Jonathon Booty is the younger brother of Josh Booty, who played quarterback on the 2003 national champion LSU Tigers. Nader's team lost a hard-fought game, 7–5, but he dominated play on the line of scrimmage, recording four sacks, two batted passes, a fumble recovery and a forced fumble. All told, in eight games he played his senior season, Nader recorded four sacks, 76 tackles, two interceptions and five knocked down passes. *Prep Football Report* ranked him the eighth-best defensive lineman in the country. Nader excelled against excellent talent. We zeroed in on him to shore up depth of our defensive line heading into the 2004 season.

Early in the process of recruiting Nader, we were competing against Michigan State, Colorado, Florida State and Tennessee. He visited all four schools, as well as Ohio State, and by mid-January he had eliminated Michigan State and Colorado. Feedback we received after his official visits to Tennessee and Florida State told us our chances were very good. Our chances were good because one of the primary factors in determining where Nader would play was the size and influence of the Arab population in that particular community. I sensed we had an advantage because, for a city its size, Columbus, Ohio, has a large and very socially and politically active Arab population.

I also realized early in the process that Nader's eldest brother, Mazen, and father, Younes, were the decision makers of the family. Younes Abdallah immigrated to the United States from Nablus, Palestine, in the late 1970s, and became a successful small business owner, providing a good life and many opportunities for his six children. For instance, Mazen graduated with honors from Loyola University Law School, and was just beginning post-graduate work at Columbia University.

As the time for the official signing day in February was closing in, I made a final visit to the family to promote Ohio State and, hopefully, land a recruit. The day after I arrived, I spent the morning visiting Nader at school with Archbishop Rummel head coach Jay Roth. While there, I also spoke with the athletic director, principal, several of Nader's teachers, as well as the other two key people of any high school, the main secretary and custodian. Each conversation only reinforced my enthusiasm and respect for this young man and his family. It also fueled my desire to see Nader become an Ohio State Buckeye. After visiting the school, I drove back to my hotel to pack. When I arrived in New Orleans I got lodging close to the city, but because I had an early flight the next day, I decided to switch to the Airport Hilton. I had several hours before a scheduled meeting at 7 P.M. with the entire Abdallah family, so I thought I had some time to catch up on phone calls. Around 1 P.M., and while I was driving to the Airport Hilton, I received a phone call from Younes, asking for a private meeting with him and Mazen before I went to their house that evening. I agreed and we set the appointment for 2 P.M. in the lobby at the Airport Hilton. Back to the previous story . . .

It was 1:45 P.M. and I was anxious. All I could think about was the fact that I'm about to meet two Arab gentlemen in 15 minutes. I had convinced myself that the Secret Service, the CIA, FBI and Homeland Security spotted me at the window and might want to interrogate me. A potential newspaper headline pounded in my brain: **"Ohio State Football Coach Arrested for Stalking President."**

"What should I do?" I thought. "I cannot abandon the two men who hold the key to whether we get an outstanding player." So, I decided to stay and do my job and face whatever consequences would arise later, if that's what the fates had planned.

I got ready and headed to the elevator with five minutes to spare. As the elevator doors were opening to the lobby, I heard something that sent shivers down my spine.

"Hey, Ohio State!" the strong male voice of man standing in front of me shouted, as he turned to yell across the lobby, "Hey, Gary, it's Ohio State."

At this point I didn't know whether to sprint, shit, crawl or put my hands in the air. Suddenly, I heard another male voice in the distance.

"Hey, Coach. Coach Conley," the voice boomed.

"Wait a minute," I thought. "I know this voice."

As I turned, I saw Gary Berry, Sr., coming at me with his hand extended to shake mine. (Berry is the father of Gary Berry, Jr., who played defensive back for Ohio State in the late 1990s and who went on to have an injury shortened NFL career. I got to know Gary Sr. when I recruited his son from DeSales High School in Columbus.)

"Coach, it's good to see you. What are you doing here?" the elder Berry inquired.

As I reminded myself to breathe, I shook his hand and he introduced me to the other government agents. What followed was truly surreal, because for the next five minutes we stood there discussing football. Each of the agents, who were dressed in dark blue suits, white shirts and dark blue ties, shared their athletic experiences; they all played football in high school, and a couple played in college. Although Gary Berry, Sr., was the only Ohio State fan among them, each of them said they cheered for the Buckeyes in the closing minutes of our double-overtime, upset victory over the Miami Hurricanes in the 2003 national championship game.

I learned that Berry's official title was "acting assistant special agent in charge of protection operations for presidential cabinet members." He was with one of President Bush's cabinet members, who accompanied the president to New Orleans. The cabinet member was at the hotel partaking in a late lunch before flying back to Washington D.C. Talk about your coincidences?

I got so caught up in the reunion and conversation with Berry that I momentarily forgot about Younes and Mazen, who at that moment were coming through the hotel's revolving front doors into the lobby. Both waved and headed in our direction; they definitely got the attention of the government agents standing near me.

Berry was the first to speak: "You know them, Coach?"

"Yes, I do," I replied, as both approached me and I made introductions. I then explained to him that I was in town recruiting Younes' son and Mazen's brother, Nader. Well, my job was done for the moment as Berry took control of the conversation. He spoke in glowing terms about Ohio State, lauding the opportunities it gave his son, both academically and athletically. He spoke about how Ohio State, while considered a football factory by critics and cynics, is really about helping student-athletes succeed as people first and foremost. I couldn't have said it better, and to this day I firmly believe Berry's testimonial helped seal the deal.

My private meeting that afternoon with Younes and Mazen lasted only about 30 minutes. The family had some specific questions it wanted answered before we met as a group later that day. Their primary concerns focused on the quality of life Nader would have at Ohio State and in Columbus, as well as the academic opportunities available to him. I once again explained about Ohio State's keen and genuine interest in helping each student-athlete earn a diploma and the academic services available to help students reach that goal. I also told them about other successful athletes, such as Eddie George, who had returned to the university during the off-season of his professional career to complete his coursework and earn a degree. After the formalities were concluded, I could tell by the way the men were looking at me that they wanted to know the whole story with the government agents. So, I explained what happened in the hotel room and my thoughts as I arrived at the lobby. Fortunately, Younes and Mazen found it as amusing as I did in hindsight.

That evening, I enjoyed a wonderful traditional Palestinian meal prepared by Nader's mother, Izzieh. I retold the story about how the day's events unfolded, and again everyone had a laugh. Then, after a couple hours of relaxed conversation, Nader told me he wanted to commit to Ohio State and join the incoming freshmen class for the fall of 2004.

Nader was red-shirted that season, and was a second-year freshman in 2005. Now listed at 6 feet 5 inches and 300 pounds in the Buckeye program, I'm convinced he will be a special player for the Buckeyes and someone the world may watch playing on Sundays in the NFL.

Na'il Diggs: So-Cal's Loss Is the Buckeyes' Gain

Sometimes gridiron tangibles—strength, speed, agility and pregame preparation—have absolutely nothing to do with a high school recruit's decision where to play college football. Sometimes fate, irony or just plain dumb luck rule the day. The story of how Ohio State snatched linebacker Na'il Ronald Diggs from the grasps of the University of Southern California in 1996 is one of those situations.

A highly coveted and nationally ranked player heading into his senior season at Dorsey High School in Los Angeles in 1995, most of the recruiting world knew Na'il had his sights set on playing at USC. He was, after all, supposed to be a Trojan. Even so, we sent letters of interest, and invited him to visit Ohio State. How could we not do so? Consider the fact that Na'il (pronounced NIE-uhl, and meaning "successful one" in Arabic) was a consensus All-America selection of *SuperPrep* his senior season. The 6 feet 3 inch, 215–pound linebacker also won All-State and All-League recognition, recording 98 tackles, including 9½ sacks and 29½ for loss, plus two safeties, helping his team to a 4–A state championship as a senior, and a two-year team record of 23–4. Na'il earned three letters in football as a defensive end, linebacker, tight end and punter. He also lettered once as a member of the high school baseball team. As you can see, pursuing this special athlete was a no-brainer.

Na'il—through his sister and guardian, Roslyn Berry— politely declined our initial requests, saying he did not want to play so far from home. (Roslyn had been Na'il's legal guardian since 1992, when his mother, Anna Faye, passed away. He was 13 when his mother died.) Also, since moving to Los Angeles from Phoenix, Na'il had become a "So-Cal" guy. In addition, his sister was employed by USC as a major gifts fundraiser. She also lived with Charlie Parker, then the Trojan's head basketball coach. As a bonus, USC allegedly promised Na'il that he could wear the No. 55 jersey, his prep football and high school number. It was as if there was an impenetrable, one-way tunnel from Na'il's home to USC, or so it seemed.

I'll never forget an afternoon in February 1996, when Ohio State head coach John Cooper interrupted a defensive staff meeting to tell us he received a call from a woman named Roslyn Berry regarding her brother, Na'il Diggs. She wanted to know if Ohio State was still interested in recruiting him. "Wow," I thought. Because it is virtually impossible for a Division I head coach to know every single recruit, Coach Cooper probably got the hint that this guy was special when we simultaneously jumped out of our seats and yelled for him to call her back . . . immediately! We not only wanted to stress that we were still very interested, we also had to find out more about what was going on with USC. We thought Na'il had signed his letter of intent the day before.

We worked quickly to determine that we still had one scholarship remaining due to an ineligibility issue with another player. Knowing this, I called Roslyn with the news, and invited Na'il to pay an official visit. Not long into that conversation curiosity got the best of me, and I inquired as to what happened with USC. The following is how Roslyn relayed the turn of events to me:

As we presumed, Na'il had signed his letter of intent, and placed it on the desk of USC athletic director Mike Garrett for his signature. Garrett had not gotten to Na'il's letter, however, because he was preoccupied with announcing to the press that he had fired Charlie Parker that morning, and was hiring Henry Bibby as interim head coach. (Parker only had the head coaching position for several months, having replaced George Rauling, who was killed in an auto accident.) Understandably, the news of Parker's dismissal did not sit well with Roslyn, who marched into Garrett's office and snatched the letter from his desk and tore it up. Here is where coincidence and irony come into play, and the story gets even more interesting.

It seems that earlier in her professional career, Roslyn worked for the athletic department at Arizona State University. At that time, the head football coach was none other than John Cooper. In addition, Charlie Parker was a native of Columbus, Ohio, played college basketball at Findlay University and was a graduate assistant coach and head coach at Bowling Green State University and Wayne State University, respectively, early in his coaching career. It's like destiny intended for Na'il to become a Buckeye.

Na'il signed with the Buckeyes, red-shirted his freshman season, but then exploded onto the college football scene in his first season as linebacker in 1997. That year, he captured first-team All-Big Ten Conference honors from the league's coaches after leading the No. 2–ranked Buckeyes in tackles for loss with 16, while finishing second on the team in both total tackles (80) and sacks (six).

Na'il went on to become a three-time letterman at Ohio State, starting his final two seasons at strong-side linebacker. He was a two-time All-Big Ten honoree, and received All-America recognition in 1999.

As a Buckeye, Na'il totaled 202 tackles (144 solo), including 18 sacks and 39 for loss, one interception, four forced fumbles, three fumble recoveries, five passes deflected, and one defensive touchdown in three seasons. He led the Buckeyes in tackles for loss twice (1998 and 1999), in sacks on two occasions (1997 and 1999), and one time in total tackles (1999) and once in forced fumbles (1999).

In his final season with Ohio State in 1999, Na'il earned first-team All-America recognition from *Football News*, third team from the *Associated Press,* and was a semi-finalist for the

Butkus Award, which is presented annually to the nation's best linebacker.

Na'il declared for the NFL draft with one year of eligibility remaining with Ohio State, and was selected by the Green Bay Packers as the first of three fourth-round choices (ninety-eighth overall) in the 2000 draft.

As he did in college, Na'il made an immediate impression in the NFL, earning a starting spot at strong-side linebacker as a rookie, beating out veteran Anthony Harris early in the preseason, to fill the spot opened by the release of incumbent George Koonce. Na'il earned All-Rookie honors that year.

Now 6 feet 4 inches and 237 pounds, Na'il entered his fifth season with the Packers in 2004 needing just 20 tackles to reach the 400-career tackle mark. A durable player, Na'il had made 50 consecutive starts over three seasons despite injuries, which is the most by a Packers' linebacker since John Anderson in 1981–86.

In 2003, in his first year at weak-side (or "Will" linebacker) Na'il posted his second straight 100-tackle season, finishing second on the team with 123 stops and leading the defense with 11 tackles for loss.

The following is what Packers linebacker's coach Mark Duffner stated about Na'il on the Packers Web site prior to the 2004 season:

"Going into his fifth year (2004), he has the demeanor of a 10-year player. Aside from being a starter, he's versatile and bright and has the pride to know that we may count on him in other spots and he takes it upon himself to understand and know assignments of those players."

Duffer continued: "I'm impressed with him as a person. He's a good man and a bright guy. Football and this organization are very important to him and that's demonstrated by his actions. He's not a bunch of words, he's a bunch of action is what he is."

Interestingly enough, Na'il demonstrated these same qualities as a high school player, which made him even more special as a recruit and then as a Buckeye. By the way, Na'il, who now calls Phoenix home, earned a bachelor's degree in aviation and plans to enter airport management after completing his career as a professional football player.

The story of Na'il Diggs is far from being concluded on many fronts, but one in particular demonstrates the power of relationships forged by the Buckeye family, which served as a bridge between our stories in this chapter. Gary Berry, Jr., was not only a teammate of Na'il's for the Buckeyes, Berry also was chosen by Green Bay in the fourth round of the 2000 NFL draft. Na'il and Berry played together that season before Berry's professional career was cut short by a neck injury in the fifth game of their mutual rookie season. In addition to being teammates, Na'il became Berry's uncle via marriage. How so, you ask? It happened when Na'il's sister, Roslyn, married Gary Berry, Sr., in August 1999. Even though the couple is no longer together, it sort of puts a whole new twist on the concept of "family" when referring to a team, don't you think?

Andy Katzenmoyer (#45) sacks the Rice quarterback in a 70–7 victory in 1996.

Chris Gamble (#7) makes a reception for a touchdown in a 45–17 victory over Indiana in 2002.

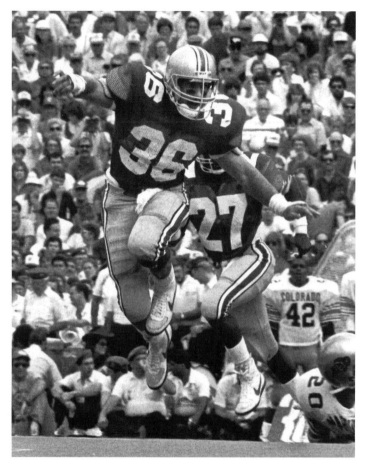

Chris Spielman (#36) in pursuit in a game versus Colorado in 1986.

Cie Grant (#6) pressures Miami Hurricane quarterback Ken Dorsey on the final play of the national championship game played in Tempe, Arizona on January 3, 2003.

Head coach John Cooper and quarterback Joe Germaine (#7)
hold the Rose Bowl trophy after a 20–17 victory over Arizona
State on January 1, 1997.

Cris Carter (#2) makes a reception between two Texas A&M
defenders in a 28–12 victory in the Cotton Bowl on
January 1, 1987.

"Big Daddy" Dan Wilkinson (#72) rushes the Wisconsin quarterback in a 14–14 tie in 1993.

Nader Abdallah (#93) waits for the huddle break in his first
game versus Miami of Ohio in the Horseshoe in 2005.

Eddie George (#27) on one of his record-breaking carries versus Illinois in a 43–3 victory in 1995. George ran for 314 yards and two touchdowns on his way to winning the Heisman Trophy.

Head coach Earle Bruce accepts the Cotton Bowl trophy on behalf of the Buckeyes in 1987.

Head coach Jim Tressel holds up the Circuit City National
Championship Trophy after the Buckeyes' 31–24 victory over
the Miami Hurricanes on January 3, 2003.

Luke Fickell (#99), Mike Vrabel (#94) and Matt Finkes (#92)
await the Penn State offense in a 38–7 victory in 1996.

Place kicker Mike Nugent (#85) and holder Andy Groom (#18)
give the Buckeyes a field goal in a 31–28 victory over
Minnesota in 2001.

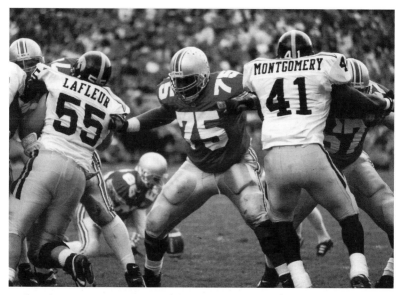

Orlando Pace (#75) provides protection in a 56–35 victory
over the Iowa Hawkeyes in 1995.

Terry Glenn (#83) makes a reception against Notre Dame in a
45–26 victory in 1995.

Michigan head coach Bo Schembechler (left) and Ohio State head coach Woody Hayes meet at mid-field prior to one of their famous gridiron battles.

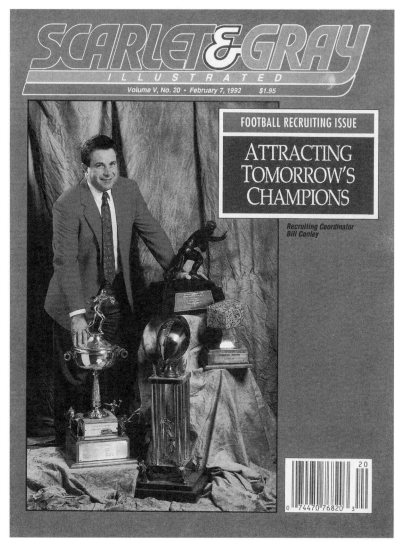

It was an honor to be recognized by *Scarlet & Gray* magazine
in 1992. That year our recruiting class was ranked No. 2 in
the country, and included players such as Eddie George,
Bobby Hoying, Kory Stringer and Craig Powell.

Ohio State Buckeyes Put In New Claim For No. 1 Rating

By JOE MOOSHIL
Associated Press Sports Writers

The proud Buckeyes of Ohio State will take a glittering record into the Rose Bowl against Stanford New Year's Day.

Ohio State climaxed a magnificent season by whipping Michigan 20-9 Saturday to finish with the Big Ten championship and a 9-0 record.

But there's more behind the record and the score. Two years ago, the Buckeyes came up with a group of sophomores who won the national championship and went on to a 27-16 Rose Bowl victory over Southern California.

Fortified with these credentials, the Buckeyes stormed toward a second unbeaten season, only to be upset by Michigan 24-12 in their final game of the 1969 campaign.

Still respected, the Buckeyes were ranked No. 1 in the Associated Press poll at the start of the current season. But as they won, the Buckeyes kept slipping in the rankings and last week dropped into fifth place behind Michigan.

The Buckeyes then couldn't have cared less. They made no bones about the fact that they were pointing for Michigan. Saturday they achieved their revenge and put in a new claim to No. 1 ranking.

Ohio State's victory over Michigan completely resolved the Rose Bowl question. Hours after the game had ended, the Big Ten office announced that the Buckeyes had been selected and had accepted.

Almost forgotten was Northwestern's forlorn Rose Bowl hopes contingent upon a Michigan State 23-20 to finish with a 6-1 conference record and a second place tie with Michigan. Iowa may have salvaged the job of Coach Ray Nagle with a 22-16 triumph over Illinois.

Iowa stopped Illinois on the one-foot line as the final gun went off. The loss almost certainly means the loss of his job for Illini Coach Jim Valek, who had been on the ropes since midseason.

Purdue saved a little face with a 40-0 triumph over Indiana in the battle for the Old Oaken Bucket. Wisconsin, the team of the future, raced away with a 39-14 victory over Minnesota.

In the Rose Bowl, Ohio State will take on Stanford whose season-ending 22-14 defeat by California gave the Indians an 8-3 record.

Nevertheless, Stanford is a foe to be feared. Indian quarterback Jim Plunkett has broken records not only in the Pacific-8 Conference but right on through the NCAA.

Ohio State enters the Rose Bowl with a team that has forged a 27-1 record over the last three seasons.

The Buck Cheer

William Conley (72) and other members of the Ohio State team leap with joy as the gun ends the game with Michigan Saturday in Columbus. The joy was for their 20-9 victory and trip to the Rose Bowl. Both teams were undefeated going into the game and the victory was revenge for the Buckeyes, who had their undefeated streak broken by Michigan last year. (AP Wirephoto)

Yes, that's me celebrating our 20-9 victory over Michigan in 1970.

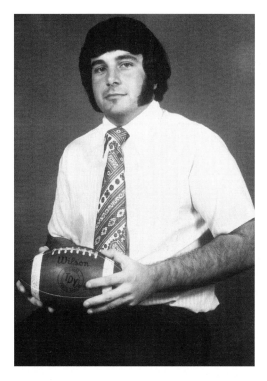

My school photo (left) when I was named head coach at London High School. (Don't ya love the lamb chops sideburns?)

I now criss-cross the country on speaking engagements. (below).

Conley leaving Buckeyes

Renowned recruiting coordinator assembled some of OSU's top classes

By Tim May
THE COLUMBUS DISPATCH

Bill Conley, Ohio State's acclaimed recruiting coordinator and tight ends coach, announced his resignation yesterday after a 17-year run, though he isn't quite gone yet.

"It's more or less a timing aspect, but I just felt in my gut this was the time," Conley said.

OSU assistant coaches' contracts run April 1 through March 31, which prompted the decision to be made by yesterday. It also was the first day of spring drills for the Buckeyes, so Conley volunteered his services through the April 24 spring game.

"We wish him nothing but the best, and we're going to miss him like crazy," coach Jim Tressel said. "I told him he can't leave until April 25, though."

Conley, 53, said he wants to make a career move after 33 years as a high school or college coach. He said he plans to choose from three opportunities in central Ohio in the next few weeks.

He became the third coach to leave Tressel's staff in the last four months. Three-year defensive coordinator Mark Dantonio was named head coach at Cincinnati in December, and 10-year running backs coach Tim Spencer took the same job with the NFL's Chicago Bears in February.

While shuffling his staff, Tressel hired Darrell Hazell from Rutgers as receivers coach and elevated his older brother Dick Tressel from associate director of football operations to be running backs coach. Now there is another spot to fill.

> **"It's tough on us, to be honest with you, because Bill is outstanding at what he does, and he bleeds scarlet and gray and he loves the kids."**
>
> **JIM TRESSEL**
> on Bill Conley

"It's tough on us, to be honest with you, because Bill is outstanding at what he does, and he bleeds scarlet and gray and he loves the kids," Tressel said. "He's one of those fixtures where you didn't have to worry about what he was assigned to do. He was going to do it."

What he did more than anything was help former coach John Cooper rebuild recruiting ties in-state when Conley was rehired from Dublin High School in 1991. Conley, a 1972 graduate of OSU, where he had walked on and played for Woody Hayes, previously had been linebackers coach for Earle Bruce from 1984 to 1987.

"In a way, it's the end of an era at Ohio State," *Ohio Football Recruiting News* publisher Bill Kurelic said. "I expect Ohio State to continue to recruit well, but there is no question he led the way for some great classes."

The players didn't know about Conley's decision until Tressel told them at the end of practice.

"I'm as shocked as anybody," junior tight end Ryan Hamby said. "I honestly thought I was going to be 40 years old trying to send my kid here and he'd still be here coaching. But he's a good man, and all I can say is I wish him the best."

MIKE MUNDEN | DISPATCH

Bill Conley says goodbye to the players after his resignation as OSU's recruiting coordinator and tight ends coach.

Conley not only coached six All-Americans — linebackers Chris Spielman and Pepper Johnson, defensive ends Matt Finkes and Mike Vrabel, punter Andy Groom and kicker Mike Nugent — he also was primarily responsible for the rise in popularity of OSU's summer camp. It has grown from an enrollment 10 years ago of about 400 to nearly 4,000 last year.

He said he's going to miss all of it.

"Very much; *very* much," Conley said, tearing up. "But like I told the players, I will always be a Buckeye."

tmay@dispatch.com

Columbus learns of my decision to retire from coaching at Ohio State after 17 seasons.

Here's the Buckeye coaching staff prior to our run for the National Championship in 2002.

My "Middletown Boys" as Buckeyes with Head Coach Earle Bruce, including from left to right (top) Cris Carter (No. 2), Deedee Howard (No. 53), Jon Peterson (No. 75), (bottom) Dwight Smith (No. 20), Sean Bell (No. 3), and Sonny Gordon (No. 7).

Conley's Recruiting Commandments

VI. Make it tough to say "No."

Make your program the standard by which a recruit compares all others. The better the relationship the recruiting coach has with the recruit the better his chance of landing him. Telephone calls, unofficial visits to campus, visits to summer football camps and written correspondence are all ways a good recruiter strengthens the coach/recruit relationship.

Ohio State assistant coach Jim Heacock is one of the best recruiters in the country. He has recruited players such as Michael Jenkins, A.J. Hawk and Tim Anderson. He keeps in constant contact with his recruits, and develops a great rapport with not only the recruit, but also their parents. He makes it difficult for them to say they may go somewhere other than Ohio State.

The 1997 coaching staff from left to right (kneeling) Jim Heacock, Chuck Stobart, Mike Jacobs, Head Coach John Cooper, Fred Pagac, Dave Kennedy, Tim Salem and Me. (standing) Tim Patillo, John Hill, Tim Spencer, John Tenuta, Bill Myles, Shawn Sims, Dave Everson and Jim Caldwell.

The NCAA:
The 800-Pound
Guerilla

College football is a sport, a business, an entertainment medium and many will say, "a way of life." How did it get this way? Why did it get this way? What have been some of the major factors that have brought changes in this truly American phenomenon? All are appropriate questions. To understand the magnitude of the phenomenon that is college football is to understand its roots. By examining the history of the game, I've come to the conclusion that there have been several monumental events over the past 100 years that not only have shaped the game of college football, but all intercollegiate athletics and their impact on society.

Until the early 1900s, college athletics were barely regulated, and many experts agree that it would have stayed this way if it weren't for the rugged nature of a new game called football. Numerous injuries—even deaths—brought about by the severe nature of the game prompted cries to abolish the game from some segments of society. Gang tackling, chopping the knees, the "flying wedge play" and the "close line" tackle were looked upon by some as barbaric and dangerous. In response to these outcries, many institutions did indeed discontinue the game. In fact, it was the death of Ohio State player John Sigirst in a game versus Western Reserve on October 26, 1901, that prompted the U.S. Congress to pass legislation regulating the sport.

Fortunately, President Theodore Roosevelt saw the positives of this hard-nosed game, and it appealed to his tough demeanor. Being a smart politician, Roosevelt also recognized that reforms were necessary to quiet objecting voices. So, he organized a summit in 1905, calling together leaders in collegiate athletics from across the nation to the White House to make changes to the sport and begin writing rules that all teams would be required to follow. By March 1906, after several more meetings and much debate, the International Athletic Association of the United States (IAAUS) was born. In 1910, the name of that organization was changed to the National Collegiate Athletic Association, or the NCAA.

The NCAA was not only a rule development and enforcement body, but by 1921 it also sponsored the first collegiate national championship. That championship, ironically, was not in football—the sport that was the impetus for its existence—but track. Interestingly enough, it would take the NCAA another 80 years to produce a true national champion in Division I-A football.

The Sanity Code

Though formation of the NCAA brought some uniformity to the sport of football, in terms of rules and execution of the game, it became painfully apparent that not every college or university was playing by the same standards off the field. It was as if there were as many ways to handle recruiting, academic eligibility, player transfers and scholarship distribution as there were programs. As a result, in January 1948, the NCAA adopted what became referred to as the "Sanity Code." This code covered five primary areas the NCAA believed needed to be modified, refined and standardized, including the definition of amateurism, academic qualifications, financial aid, recruiting and the role colleges and universities must play in controlling their athletic departments. In 1950, the "Byrd Resolution" took the code a step further by standardizing policies based on enrollment.

The "Sanity Code" is recognized as the first step by the NCAA to bring "common sense" to intercollegiate competition. Many pieces of legislation would follow in an attempt to "level the playing field" in college athletics. Although specific policies would change many times over throughout the next half century, the "Sanity Code" still speaks for itself.

Television Rights

One of the most sweeping influences on college football, and arguably the biggest influence on the sport, was the advent of television. In fact, the NCAA was initially apprehensive of the medium, and in 1951 declared a "moratorium" on live telecasts of football games. The NCAA feared television would hurt attendance at games, taking away a lucrative activity on college campuses. However, one year later the NCAA modified its official position by allowing colleges to have one game televised per season. The NCAA devised the "Television Plan of 1952," the same year the National Broadcasting Company (NBC) paid more than $1 million for the rights to televise football that year. Feeding the NCAA's stubborn and shortsighted position is the fact that football was quickly emerging as a top revenue-producing sport for colleges and universities, and it did not want to share any probable windfalls. Its fears were never realized and, in fact, were laid to waste by the fact that television only heightened the popularity of college football and drove more and more people to games to experience this growing cultural spectacle. This resulted in the construction of larger stadiums to accommodate the public demand, which only continued to feed the machine that the NCAA is today. Interestingly, the American Broadcasting Company (ABC) acquired the television rights to college football in 1966, and maintained a stranglehold on it, paying as much as $31 million to the NCAA to broadcast a single season of games. The advent of cable television in the late 1970s changed the landscape for good, opening up opportunities for more collegiate players to be recognized by the public and NFL scouts. ESPN quickly made a name for itself by broadcasting second-tier or obscure games, and found a profitable marketing niche. (Ohio State has the distinction of playing in the first college game broadcast via cable. The Buckeyes' game versus Minnesota on September 15, 1979 was broadcast on CUBE-TV during Earle Bruce's first season as head coach. Ohio State won that game 21–17.)

Title IX

One of the most controversial issues dealing with college athletics was the passage of Title IX in 1972. The crux of the federal legislation was to prohibit discrimination in education, and therefore, intercollegiate athletics. This brought about sweeping policy changes as colleges and universities added women's sports to gain Title IX compliance. The change was a positive one for female athletes who hungered for an opportunity to compete and excel. (The first female athlete to compete in an NCAA championship was Wayne State University diver Doria Schilerm in 1973.) Few would argue against the social benefits of this legislation.

Unfortunately, the sprint for Title IX compliance brought financial hardships down on many athletic departments. Many institutions have been forced to discontinue men's sports or reduce scholarships therein to maintain balance between their men's and women's programs. It seems only the large "football power" schools, such as Ohio State—where revenue from the football program provides cash flow to maintain the athletic department—can offer a wide range of men's and women's programs. Despite this funding disparity, the number of football scholarships has been cut to maintain parity within the department.

The ironic thing about all of this is that the demand to produce a winning football program is stronger than ever. The playing field has been leveled due to scholarship limits, but the demand to win doesn't change. To the college football coach this translates into higher salaries, but higher stress and less longevity. All of this gives credence to those who argue that college football is a business, not a sport.

Proposition 48

From the onset of the "Sanity Code" of 1948, there had been a steady outcry from politicians and academicians to establish academic standards for intercollegiate athletics. These cries and the demands for reform were finally heard in 1983 with the passage of Proposition 48. Proposition 48 established a core curriculum that must be passed, along with minimum standardized test scores for student athletes to qualify for financial aid at an NCAA-affiliated institution. The core grade point average and test score index has changed several times over the past 22 years with one major consistent texture; the index and the number of core classes required have increased steadily. By 2006 the prospective student-athlete must have a minimum test score of 1010 on the SAT or an 86 on the ACT along with a minimum core-class grade point average of 2.0. If the test score is lower, the graduate's grade point average must be higher. Thus, a sliding scale is used to determine who receives a scholarship or not. At the same time, the student must have passed at least 16 core classes. In 1993, the NCAA established an Initial Eligibility Clearinghouse that analyzed each athlete's high school transcript to determine if financial aid standards had been met. Few coaches and administrators will argue the necessity of setting academic criteria to receive aid or participate in athletics. Some have stridently debated the validity of test scores, but most would be best served to prepare for ever-increasing academic standards in the future. Additionally, not only are academic standards increasing for student athletes, but colleges and universities are also under the microscope. They will soon be forced to disclose student-athlete graduation rates and will lose scholarships if they fall below minimum prescribed standards.

Bowl Championship Series (BCS)

A longtime debated issue came to a head in 1996 with the establishment of the Bowl Championship Series (BCS). For the first time since the establishment of the NCAA, there was agreement to let two Division I football teams play for the title of national champion. This decision only spawned additional questions, such as what criterion would be used to decide which two teams will play for this title? What will happen to the structure of bowl games, and will they lose their perennial prestige? How will revenues from Bowl games be disbursed?

To this day, not everyone is completely happy with the championship formula. And I suspect no one will ever be completely happy, even if Division I football went to a playoff system similar to the one that determines the Division I-AA national champion. Even so, there are many coaches and football pundits that fervently believe a Division I playoff would never work. What I do know is that modifications to the current system will continue to be made and that this system will never be perfect. Can a playoff be constructed and be successful? Maybe. Whatever happens, I do believe that the popularity of college football will only continue to increase, and that the annual debates over which team is the "real" national champion fuels this popularity. It reminds me of a trick often used in television series to create a popular character that no one ever sees. The character, Maris Crane, of the long-running, NBC hit "Frasier" is a primary example of this creative technique. Viewers never got to see the elusive Maris, but she was well known and much debated throughout the run of the show. Now, I am not suggesting the NCAA was aware of this when it established the BCS. No, that would give way too much credit to the powers that manage this 800-pound guerilla. What I am suggesting is that an imperfect system is spawning just enough creative tension to heighten interest and intrigue, and grow the popularity of the sport.

Thank You, Teddy!

The sport of football owes much to President Theodore Roosevelt. A more passive president—such as Woodrow Wilson—might have sided with those who believe it was too violent and too dangerous and served no purpose in polite society. I like to believe there is a reason this issue came to a head under the Rough Rider. A hundred years have passed since football received its stay of execution, and while the rules have been altered through the century, the passion for the game has not waned. Thank God, and thank Teddy!

Conley's Recruiting Commandments

VII. It's all academic.

Ineligible recruits make for unemployed coaches. Success in recruiting is greater when academic and athletic ability are equal.

Linebacker Greg Bellisari always had his priorities in line. He was the ideal student-athlete and a pleasure to recruit. He not only was an outstanding player, he became a captain and, most importantly, went on to the Ohio State Medical School. Today, he is known as Greg Bellisari, M.D.

Big (6 feet 7 inches and 325 pounds), strong, fast, agile and tough, Orland Pace is considered to be the best offensive tackle to ever play the game. He's also intelligent, caring and very civically minded.

The Golden Age
of Buckeye
Recruiting

(The John Cooper Era)

The writing was on the wall for me at Ohio State following the cold and calloused firing of Earle Bruce six days before the Michigan game in 1987. Sure, there was a slim chance the new head coach, whomever it may be, would retain some of Earle's assistants, but history wasn't on my side. So, I began looking for a new job while waiting to hear just who would be the next Buckeye head coach.

On December 31, 1987, former OSU athletic director Jim Jones announced that Arizona State University head coach John Cooper would be the twenty-first head coach in Buckeye football history. I did not know John Cooper personally at the time, but his coaching reputation preceded him. In coaching terms, "Coop" was a hot commodity, and luring him to Ohio State was considered a huge coup by those who made themselves believe the Buckeyes had grown stale under Earle. (Funny, Earle Bruce had a .755 winning percentage when he was fired, and that mark still places him in second place among all Buckeye head coaches behind the man he replaced, the legendary Woody Hayes. Tell me, at what point did winning football games become stale? Stale, my ass. Earle Bruce was a winner and a loyal Buckeye, and this decision goes down on my list of "Most Inept Athletic Administration Decisions.")

Despite my personal feelings at that time, John Cooper would become the Buckeye's new field general, and for good reason. With an overall record as a head coach of 82–40–2 prior to accepting the Ohio State position, Cooper had a reputation for "breathing new life" into programs. He did so at his first head coaching job at Tulsa between 1977 and 1984, where he lead the Golden Hurricanes to six-consecutive winning seasons, including five-consecutive Missouri Valley Conference championships.

Cooper had similar success at Arizona State between 1985 and 1987, leading his first Sun Devil team to an 8–4 record and a berth in the Holiday Bowl. A loss on the last Saturday of the regular season cost ASU its first-ever PAC-10 football championship that year. The next year, the Sun Devils would make history and successfully exorcise the previous year's demons by winning the elusive conference title, and making their first-ever trip to Pasadena, where they capped off a storybook season with a win over Michigan in the Rose Bowl on January 1, 1986. Despite heavy graduation losses that year, ASU went to a school-record, third-consecutive bowl game in 1987. A win over Air Force in the Freedom Bowl sealed a 7–4–1 season.

As for me, I knew I had no place on Cooper's staff because of my short stint at Ohio State and the fact that we had no common friends or colleagues. So, in the spring of 1988, I accepted a teaching position and job as head coach at Dublin High School in Dublin, Ohio—a fast-growing, affluent Columbus suburb. I would remain with the Shamrocks for three seasons, amassing an 18–12 record, before returning to Ohio State to join Cooper's staff prior to the 1991 season.

I guess I always knew in my heart that I would return to college football at some point; I just did not know when. Also, at that moment at age 37, a part of me sincerely felt that if I did not return to the college ranks, it wouldn't necessarily be a tragedy. I truly enjoyed coaching high school football, where you have more of an influence on the development of the athlete as a person. At the Division I college level, an assistant football coach is merely a spoke in a massive wheel, whereas a head high school coach is the hub.

How and why did Ohio State come knocking again?

If you did not already know it, John Cooper had a rather rough beginning to his tenure at Ohio State. Not only was he a "non-Buckeye," he also wasn't a "Woody" disciple like Bruce. Cooper also turned some people off because he spoke with a smooth, southern drawl, which belied his Tennessee birthright. If that wasn't enough, he also was among the first generation of a new breed of marketing-conscious, CEO-like coaches. Some in the hallowed halls at Ohio State and beyond didn't believe it was dignified for a football coach to be doing grocery store and hot tub commercials.

To make matters worse is the fact that Cooper did not have the most auspicious start on the field in 1988, recording a 4–6–1 record, including a loss to Michigan. Now don't get me wrong, most Buckeye fans will forgive a coach for one losing season; they'll even forgive one loss to those damned Wolverines. But when it becomes habit, well, you've got a lot of explaining to do. Cooper's 2–10–1 career record against Michigan over 13 seasons as head coach will forever remain his Achilles' heel, and something for which some fans will never forgive him.

This is unfortunate and unfair to John Cooper as a human being and as a coach. Many fans choose to forget the fact that, after that first losing season, Cooper's teams amassed 10 consecutive winning seasons and averaged nine wins a year. Some also choose to forget that, during the 1990s, no other head coach had more players win individual honors for their performances on the playing field and in the classroom. A virtual "Who's Who from Ohio State" during the Cooper era still peppers the ranks of the National Football League, and some of those players are destined for the Pro Football Hall of Fame. Others choose to forget the fact that Cooper is only the second coach in Ohio State football history to eclipse the 100-win plateau. OSU finished the 1990s with 91 wins—one of just two Big Ten schools to win at least 90 games, and a feat that was the seventh-best win total among Division I-A schools for the decade. With an Ohio State record of 111–43–4, Cooper would finish his Buckeye coaching career as the third-winningest coach in OSU history, trailing only Woody Hayes and Earle Bruce in winning percentage. Cooper also has the third longest coaching tenure at Ohio State behind Hayes and Dr. John W. Wilce, who coached for 16 years between 1913 and 1928.

To some, Cooper was an outsider that never understood Ohio State, even though he has a record of which any coach would be proud. Efforts to alter this perception are one of the reasons I was asked to rejoin the Buckeye coaching staff in 1991 as recruiting coordinator. You see, Cooper was beginning to have limited success on the field at that time, but there were some who believed Ohio's premiere collegiate football program was losing too many talented Ohio-bred players to other schools, including Michigan. My name was suggested to Cooper because of my longtime ties with Ohio high school coaches, as well as various relationships I had built during my time coaching with Earle Bruce. So, once again my life jumped onto another road . . . and what a ride it was!

I deeply respect John Cooper as a coach and as a person. He was an assistant coach's head coach, meaning he allowed and trusted the good people he had around him to do their jobs. Even so, Cooper was not nearly as hands off as some people are quick to criticize, and he was quite capable of being decisive when necessary. The fact that he was such a good person contributed to the fact that he was sometimes slow to make tough decisions, and that came back to haunt him. Other times, he was right on target.

A good example of John Cooper stepping in to make the tough decision was prior to the 1997 Rose Bowl versus none other than Arizona State. The 1996 season, which saw the Buckeyes win a share of the Big Ten title with an 11–1 record, was unique in that the Buckeyes platooned its starting quarterbacks. Senior Stanley Jackson started every game that season, with back-up Joe Germaine playing a critical role off the bench at strategic moments in games. Jackson and Germaine had vastly contrasting styles of play. Jackson was the quintessential athlete-quarterback who possessed great running speed and agility in addition to being a sprintout passer. Germaine, on the other hand, was a prototypical drop-back passing quarterback who was quite skilled at reading defensive coverages and making great decisions under pressure.

During the weeks leading up to the Rose Bowl, the Buckeye coaching staff was divided about which player should start at quarterback. Some were pushing for Germaine, a junior, because he had the hot hand at the end of the season; he even started the Michigan game. Others argued the team should ride the horse that got it to that point, and that horse was Stanley Jackson, who had won every game he started that year. Ultimately, John Cooper stepped in and gave the start to Jackson, who played well in the Buckeyes' 20–17 win. Despite Jackson's steady play, many Buckeye and college football fans will never forget Germaine's heroism in the final 1:40 of the game. Coming off the bench as usual, Germaine guided the team 65 yards in 12 plays, throwing a five-yard pass to wide-out David Boston to take the lead with 19 seconds remaining on the game clock. It's the kind of performance many young athletes dream about when they are growing up . . . to be in control of your team's destiny at the end of the game and making the plays to secure the win.

One of the things I admired most about John Cooper was his ability to be the head football coach at a place like Ohio State and still maintain the human qualities that most people either put on hold or eliminate. The qualities I'm talking about are the devotion he showed his family and the time he made for them during the crazy in-season months. I also admired the ability he had to get away from "the game" to enjoy much-loved hobbies like hunting, fishing and playing golf. I've always said that if you spend just one hour with John Cooper, you know exactly where he stands in relation to football and life. John Cooper is honest, open and incredibly and sometimes ridiculously frugal. The latter quality he admits stems from his days growing up in a working-class family in eastern Tennessee. The son of a carpenter who often struggled to provide enough for his family, Cooper often jokes that he lived so far in the woods that he had to head toward town to go hunting, or that he was so poor he was 14 before he realized that macaroni wasn't a meat.

John got into trouble early on because he didn't understand the socio-political machine that is Ohio State Football. And because he was so disarmingly honest with his players, coaches, fans and the media, some people viewed him as uncaring and aloof. Again, these are not the traits I saw in John Cooper. Unfortunately, Cooper learned the hard way after being burned a number of times in the media, causing him to become more guarded in public, which only fueled more rumor, suspicion and innuendo.

I am often asked what event or events ultimately lead to John Cooper's downfall at Ohio State. Within the ranks of Ohio State, it seem apparent that Andy Geiger, the new athletic director, was getting impatient with Cooper's record in bowl games and against Michigan, and not necessarily in that order. What I do know is that about the middle of Cooper's final season in 2000, support from certain administrators of the athletic department seemed to dry up. The air was thick and it was like a time bomb set to go off, and there was no way of controlling it.

The proverbial explosion occurred after we lost the Outback Bowl to South Carolina on January 1, 2001. It was a devastating loss to the same Lou Holtz we had beaten soundly in 1995 and 1996 when he coached at Notre Dame. Even though we had opportunities to win the Outback Bowl, we did not get it done. It was literally a team loss; this means we could have had better leadership from players and we could have coached better that day. We could have and should have played with more emotion, but the day belonged to the Gamecocks, who wanted the win more than we did. That game still leaves a sour taste in my mouth. It made a hero of Ryan Brewer, a player from Troy, Ohio, who was never recruited by Ohio State. I'm sure that fact above all others motivated him to play what may have been the best game of his life. Even though he hadn't been heavily recruited and wasn't a full-time starter for South Carolina, he was phenomenal that day. It was a game of a lifetime for a fine young man, and I'm sure he's still quite proud of his performance . . . and he has every right to be proud because he was the best player on the field that given day.

After that game, the flight home seemed long and agonizing; you could have heard a pin drop on the airplane as players and coaches barely spoke out loud. In hindsight, I think we all knew what could happen, and what would transpire over the next 48 hours. That's college football, and as a player and coach you must be prepared to handle the bad along with the good elements. The following day, I was in my office early as usual, working on the recruiting schedule for the next month. Shortly after I arrived, I heard John Cooper open the door of his office. I don't recall the time frame, but it didn't seem long before I saw Andy Geiger coming out of Cooper's office, and it was obvious by the look on his face that it hadn't been a cordial visit. After Geiger left the building, I walked down to Cooper's office, closed the door behind me and sat down in a chair in front of his desk. He was pale and tense, and with a blank expression on his face, he muttered, "We're gone." Kaboom! The bomb exploded. None of us knew what fate awaited us until the next head coach was hired.

One thing was for sure, the athletic administration that once was so supportive, became cold as ice and very bureaucratic in the way they treated all of us, especially John Cooper. Even though I wasn't necessarily surprised by this posture, it still seemed a bit cruel and insensitive when you consider the personal sacrifices and grueling hours coaches put in to build a successful program. But I had seen it before with Earle Bruce; the "powers that be" at Ohio State got their way and the John Cooper era was over.

Even though his tenure as head coach ended ungracefully, John Cooper accomplished much at Ohio State. He coached great players and great teams during his reign. His rosters read like an Ohio State All-Star team and include first-team All-Americans, such as Steve Tovar, the late Korey Stringer, Dan Wilkinson, Eddie George, Terry Glenn, Orlando Pace, Mike Vrabel, Shawn Springs, Andy Katzenmoyer, Rob Murphy, Antoine Winfield, David Boston, Damon Moore and Na'il Diggs. Those players also earned All-Big Ten honors, and were joined by other high-profile players, including Alan Kline, Jason Simmons, Alonzo Spellman, Jeff Graham, Joey Galloway, Gary Berry, Jr., Tim Williams, Lorenzo Styles, Rickey Dudley, Bobby Hoying, Matt Finkes, Brent Bartholomew, Eric Gohlstine, Joe Germaine, Michael Wiley and Ahmed Plummer. Additionally, and maybe even more impressive, is the fact that 65 players during Cooper's tenure earned Academic All-Big Ten accolades.

A Golden Era

I call the John Cooper years at Ohio State the Golden Era, and if all the facts are considered this contention bears fruit. Not only did his tenure include some great players, as mentioned above, but those players also were part of some great teams. I've always maintained that it takes four things for a team to win a national championship. The first thing is having enough talent to get the job done. The second is being able to keep that talent healthy. The third involves the ability of the coaching staff to mold that talent into an effective and efficient machine. And the fourth is having some good luck along the way. A dropped pass, a missed field goal, a fumble, or a blown open field tackle can mean the difference of a win or loss in a game and a chance to compete for the national crown. Those elements, which are ultimately out of the control of coaches, also can determine the longevity and legacy of a head coach and his staff.

Under John Cooper, the Ohio State football team recorded some of their greatest victories as well as some of their most devastating defeats. Some of the very best Buckeye teams in history took the field during these years. Consider the 1993, 1995, 1996 and 1998 teams. All of these teams were one regular season victory of being undefeated and possibly playing for a national title. Unfortunately, losses to Michigan and in some bowl games will forever tarnish the memories of those great seasons. You may be asking whether these teams had less of a desire to win than the 2002 national championship team? I know that's not true. Did the 2002 national championship team possess better individual talent? Many, including myself, would argue against that statement when you compare the rosters. These debates may be moot, but you have to wonder what would the legacy of John Cooper be if his teams had just a little more luck along the way? For those of you who still do not believe that John Cooper is a true Buckeye, I must point out that he could have lived anywhere after his retirement from coaching, but he decided to live in Columbus, Ohio. (By the way, the athletic director who fired John moved to Seattle after he retired.)

An Old Rivalry Restored

One of the all-time great victories in Buckeye history occurred during John Cooper's reign. The game was the 1995 Football Classic between Ohio State and Notre Dame. Arguably two of the greatest programs in all of college football, this game was significant because these two teams had not faced one another since 1936, when the Buckeyes lost to the Fighting Irish in South Bend, Indiana, by a score of 7–2. This time, historical Ohio Stadium would be the setting for a rivalry that had lain dormant for 59 years.

Excitement surrounding the game began that spring and was at a fever pitch by the kickoff on September 30. Notre Dame had highly touted Ron Powlus at quarterback, along with a talented and lightening-quick defense. Some believed that Notre Dame would embarrass the Buckeyes at home, but Ohio State had other ideas. Even though Ohio State trailed 17–14 at halftime, it was apparent to most people that the Irish bubble was ready to burst, as they just couldn't shake a dogged Buckeye team. I can only recall a few Buckeye teams that played with the intensity and enthusiasm the 1995 team was playing with that game. (In fact, I wouldn't see this level of intensity again until the 2002 national championship game.) The performance of Buckeye quarterback Bobby Hoying overshadowed that of Powlus, as he threw for 272 yards and four touchdown passes. The Ohio State offense rolled up 533 total yards, which explains why the game took almost four hours to complete. Halfback Eddie George rushed for more than 200 yards that day to begin his march toward the Heisman Trophy. But the play of the day was made by wide receiver Terry Glenn, who raced 82 yards for a touchdown after one reception, leaving in the dust world-class sprinter Allen Rossum, who played in Notre Dame's ultra-talented secondary.

The Buckeye defense was equally impressive, causing three second-half turnovers to set up the offensive explosion. Junior linebacker Greg Bellisari recorded 12 tackles en route to a 45–26 Ohio State victory. That game would become the worse loss for a Lou Holtz—coached Notre Dame team. Interestingly, the Buckeyes would travel to South Bend the next year and avenge the 1936 loss by defeating the Irish 29–16. For two consecutive years, John Cooper had defeated Lou Holtz and the mighty Fighting Irish.

Big plays and high-profile players such as Eddie George and Terry Glenn would become synonymous with the John Cooper era. During the 1990s, in fact, the Ohio State Buckeyes won nearly every major individual award in college football, including the Heisman, Outland, Lombardi, Walter Camp, Maxwell, Butkus, Jim Thorpe and Fred Biletnikoff awards. This era produced a record number of award winners as well as a record number of players drafted by the NFL. There were so many great players that their stories alone would make for another book. I would, however, like to mention a few of the players I recruited whose stories and accomplishments set them apart.

"Big Daddy" Dan Wilkinson: Humble Beginnings

The story about how Ohio State landed Dan Wilkinson of Dayton High School in 1991 is one that epitomizes the virtues of patience and persistence in recruiting. I was hired by John Cooper in March 1991 to serve as the Buckeyes recruiting coordinator. Excited about my return to Ohio State, I decided to work during the university's spring break to get caught up on the massive amount of game tape that littered my office. You see, former recruiting coordinator Steve Pederson had left for Tennessee, leaving a huge backlog of tape that had yet to be reviewed.

I dove in, knowing that the official signing date had passed that February. My thoughts in doing so were that I might be able to identify and attract some good walk-on candidates who had not decided to play elsewhere. Near the bottom of the stack was a film on an offensive and defensive lineman from Dayton named Dan Wilkinson. As I evaluated the film, I noticed this huge lineman (6 feet 5 inches and well over 300 pounds) had very good feet. He ran well and seemed to be very powerful. The only negative I could find was that he tended to take plays off now and then. This would normally turn most college recruiters off, but then I noticed that this big man never left the field and played all 48 minutes of every game. He was definitely talented enough to play Division I football, but I had to know why he hadn't been offered a scholarship.

I called Dan's coach, Tom Montgomery, who informed me that Dan had yet to pass the ACT test, and that there was a possibility he wouldn't do so before graduation. At that point, I called Dan and told him I would stay in touch with him and to let me know if he made the test score. I didn't wait long, as Dan called me in June and told me he had passed the ACT. At that point, I conferred with Coach Cooper and we decided to offer him a scholarship. The next day, Dan and his grandmother came to campus to sign his scholarship papers. The family was of very modest means and I'll never forget Dan arriving at the meeting wearing a stained dress shirt, worn out pants, and leather dress shoes with numerous holes. No one at this juncture even thought that we were meeting a young man who, in less than three years, would be a millionaire playing in the NFL.

Dan reported to August practice tipping the scales at 375 pounds. Even though he wanted to play defense, at that weight, it would be difficult to run and pursue like a defensive lineman has to do at the Division I level. Dan would spend the 1991 season on our depth chart as an offensive tackle. He redshirted that season because we stayed injury free at that position, but he was ready if needed.

After the 1991 season, Dan asked Coach Cooper if he could play defense in the spring. Coach told him that if he lost 50 pounds (he now weighed 350 pounds) he would give him a shot. To be honest, none of us expected Dan to lose the weight, but he proved us wrong. By the time spring practice started, Dan was down to 295 pounds and he ran a sub-4.9 second 40-yard dash. He actually beat one of our starting linebackers in an after-practice race. All of us stood there with our tongues out in disbelief at how Dan had changed his body.

"Big Daddy" Dan Wilkinson became a powerful, quick defensive tackle. When he threw a forearm or made an arm rip into an opponent, it sounded like a cannon exploding. He was downright dangerous on the football field. He earned a starting position as a sophomore in 1992 and won All-Big Ten honors, recording 46 tackles, including 10.5 tackles-for-loss and 6.5 sacks. As a junior in 1993, Dan was the most dominant defensive lineman in college football, ending the year with 44 tackles and 13 tackles-for-loss. Opponents could not block Dan one-on-one, and by season's end he again won All-Big Ten laurels and was a consensus All-America pick. The Cincinnati Bengals made him a first selection in the NFL draft in April 1994, and he would leave Ohio State to continue his football career professionally.

I can't help but think about what kind of legacy Dan Wilkinson would have had at Ohio State if he stayed to play two more seasons. But I completely understand why "Big Daddy" decided to declare for the draft. A number one draft pick never has to wear stained and worn out clothing.

Terry Glenn: Sprinting Past Adversity

A Buckeye from 1993 to 1995, Terry Glenn was one of the most versatile athletes ever to play at Ohio State. Possessing great speed and quickness, Terry was a star athlete at Brookhaven High School in Columbus, where he was a three-year letter winner as a wide receiver and cornerback. He even punted and served as a return specialist. As a co-captain his senior year, Terry finished the season with 14 receptions for 416 yards (29.7 yard average) and four touchdowns and earned second-team all-district honors. Terry also lettered three years in basketball and track, plus two years in tennis. Needless to say, everyone was after Terry—the only problem was his grades. Even though he never used this as an excuse, Terry had one of the toughest situations growing up I had ever encountered. He never knew his father and his mother was killed when he was 13. Thank goodness for Charles and Mary Henley (who raised Terry and served as his legal guardians), Brookhaven head coach Gregg Miller and his teachers, all of whom took Terry under their wings. Fortunately, Terry qualified for graduation by the end of his senior year.

Unfortunately, we no longer had any scholarships available by the time Terry qualified. Growing up in the shadows of Ohio State and even selling soda at games as a youth, Terry longed to be a Buckeye. He decided to join the team as a walk-on with a commitment from the school to receive a grant-in-aid in January if he proved he could cut it in the classroom. To his credit, Terry made the grades and we kept our promise.

Terry was a three-year letter winner at Ohio State and played 32 career games with the Buckeyes, making 12 starts, and finished with 79 receptions for 1,677 yards (21.2-yard average) and 17 touchdowns. He also had six career carries for 31 yards and contributed to the return game with 18 kickoff returns for 399 yards (22.2-yard average) and five punt returns for 28 yards (5.6-yard average).

He had a standout season as a junior, receiving the Fred Biletnikoff Award, given annually to the country's top wide receiver, and earning All-America recognition. A unanimous All-Big Ten selection, he set school receiving records with 1,411 yards and 17 touchdowns on 64 receptions. Terry averaged 22.0 yards-per-reception, the highest among career Buckeyes with more than 20 catches in a season and started 12 of Ohio State's 13 games. His top collegiate game came against Pittsburgh when he set a school record with nine receptions for 253 yards (28.1-yard average) and four touchdowns. He also posted 17 rushing yards, 16 yards on punt returns and 29 yards on a kickoff return to rack up 315 total yards in a 54–14 victory over the Panthers.

The New England Patriots drafted Terry in the first round in 1996. He exploded onto the NFL scene as a rookie that year, finishing the season with a league rookie-record and team-leading 90 receptions for 1,132 yards and six touchdowns. He went on to earn AFC Rookie of the Year honors from the United Press International, was an All-Pro selection by *USA Today,* was named to the All-Rookie team of *Pro Football Weekly* and the Pro Football Writers of America, and was runner-up to former Buckeye teammate Eddie George for the Associated Press Rookie of the Year honors. He also was an All-AFC selection by UPI and was the second alternate for the 1997 Pro Bowl. Terry played for the Dallas Cowboys in 2004, in what was his tenth NFL season.

All in all, I consider all of this quite remarkable for a young man who fought through insurmountable odds to succeed. It's also a great tribute to the fine people of Brookhaven High School who selflessly gave of themselves to make sure Terry would stay on a path of success.

Orlando Pace: House of Pancakes

A graduate of Sandusky High School, in Sandusky, Ohio, Orlando Pace earned All-State honors in football and basketball. Now, you may be saying that this feat is not unusual, but I would argue it is for a young man who was 6 feet 5 inches and well over 300 pounds at that time. Massive, fast and athletic, Orlando was a hot commodity heading into his senior season in 1993. The "Big O" visited several colleges early in the recruiting process, but we knew early on that he was bound for Columbus.

Orlando earned a starting position at offensive tackle by the end of his first practice of pre-season camp and started every game for the next three years before passing up his senior season to enter the NFL draft. Now 6 feet 6 inches and 330 pounds, Orlando redefined the position of left tackle, which is arguably the most important position on the offensive line because the left tackle protects the blind side of a right-handed quarterback in pass protection. In 1994, with Orlando at left tackle and the late Korey Stringer at right tackle, the Buckeyes had two of the most dominant "bookend" linemen in all of college football.

There are four characteristics of Orlando that must be explained. First, he was a powerful blocker. In a 72–0 rout over Pitt in 1996, Orlando "pancaked" Panther defensive end Rod Humphrey numerous times. Secondly, Orlando was so athletic that he got downfield to block on a regular basis. In a 70–7 rout of Rice in 1996, Orlando led tailback Michael Wiley on a 49–yard run; he also led tailback Joe Montgomery on a 50-yard scamper against Iowa that season. Third, Orlando refused to give up sacks and never took plays off. His massive frame and long arms made it nearly impossible for defenders to get around him. In fact, he did not allow a sack in either of his last two years at Ohio State. Orlando routinely graded at 90 percent or more during his Buckeye career. Lastly, Orlando was so athletic that he also played defense in goal-line situations. He not only plugged holes, he could shuffle along the front and make plays even if opponents ran to the opposite side of him. Orlando truly defined the term "man among boys" at both the college and now at the professional level, where he is recognized as the "greatest" offensive tackle to ever play the game. Orlando endeared himself with Buckeye fans, and became well known for his "pancake" blocks, where he knocked a defender to the ground and on his back. Ohio State's Sports Information Department had fun with this image for promotional purposes by developing a magnet that resembled a stack of pancakes. They used this magnet to promote Orlando for postseason awards. The magnet even got attention by "Good Morning America." Always one with country logic, John Cooper used to quip that Orlando was so big that he was "born on July 12, 13 and 14," and so tough that he "went hunting with a switch."

Whether it was the magnet or Orlando's dominant play, he made college football history by becoming the first sophomore to win the Lombardi Award in 1995. As a junior, he again made history by becoming the first two-time winner of that trophy. He also won the Outland Trophy and finished fourth in the Heisman Trophy balloting as a junior—the highest finish by a lineman since a second-place finish by Ohio State's John Hicks in 1973. Other collegiate honors for Orlando included consensus All-Big Ten and All-America honors in both 1995 and 1996. He was the *Football News* Offensive Player of the Year and the Big Ten's Offensive Player of the Year in 1996. He also received the *Chicago Tribune's* Silver Football Award as the Most Valuable Player in the Big Ten. Orlando was the Big Ten Freshman of the Year in 1994 and the Big Ten Offensive Lineman of the Year in 1995 and 1996. He also was a finalist for the Maxwell Award in 1996.

Orlando would have to add shelves to his trophy case after leaving Ohio State to enter the NFL draft after his junior season. He was taken as the first overall pick in the 1997 NFL draft by the St. Louis Rams, where he continues to play today. Now 6 feet 7 inches and 325 pounds, Orlando has been a fixture Pro Bowl selection since 1999, when he helped lead the Rams to the Super Bowl.

Today, Orlando is as recognized for his civic and social work in and around St. Louis as he is for his gridiron skills. To me, the finest compliment that can be given to Orlando is the fact that he is as good a human being as he is a football player, and he remains one of the most humble and selfless athletes I've ever known.

Andy Katzenmoyer: The Misunderstood Warrior

Andy Katzenmoyer was one of the most talented and misunderstood athletes I've ever recruited to play at Ohio State. I know this statement may amaze, amuse and confound some of you, but not only was Andy an exceptional athlete, he also was a better student than many people give him credit for being. At issue here is that Andy made a decision before his college career began to leave early to pursue his dream of playing in the NFL, and he allowed his grades to slip. Was this a bad decision? Probably, when you place it in the grand scheme of life. But to think that Andy Katzenmoyer could not handle the academic demands at Ohio State is absolutely and unequivocally false.

Six feet 4 inches and 265 pounds, Andy came to Ohio State after a brilliant career as a linebacker and fullback, where he played for head coach Rocky Pentello at Westerville South High School, located in Westerville, Ohio, a Columbus suburb.

I was extremely excited when Andy committed to Coach Cooper and the Buckeyes early in the recruiting process at the start of his senior season in high school in 1995. Blessed with exceptional size and speed (he also lettered in track and baseball at Westerville South), Andy was a unanimous All-America selection that year, adding *USA Today* National Defensive Player of the Year, Ohio Mr. Football (the first defensive player to ever earn that honor), All-Ohio, Associated Press Ohio Division I Player of the Year, Columbus and Atlanta Touchdown Club's National Player of the Year, All-State and All-League honors as well.

The excitement and hype surrounding the son of Warren and Dianne Katzenmoyer when he arrived at Ohio State only intensified when he chose to wear No. 45, becoming the first and only player to wear this number since fabled two-time Heisman Trophy winner Archie Griffin. You would think that the hoopla surrounding an 18-year-old would have adversely affected his play, but not Andy. He seemed to be motivated by the attention.

Andy started the first game of his freshman year in 1996 and was a regular for 37 consecutive games before opting to pursue an NFL career at the end of his junior season. A ferocious hitter with running back speed, Andy would win a plethora of awards, including the Butkus Award and consensus All-America honors as a sophomore in 1997, the 1996 *Football News* and Big Ten Freshman of the Year. He was a three-time All-Big Ten selection and two-time finalist for the Lombardi Award.

Andy amassed three-year statistical totals of 197 solo tackles, 256 total tackles, 50 tackles-for-loss, 192 yards in losses, 18 quarterback sacks and six interceptions. He was twice named the team's Randy Gradishar Award winner as best linebacker (1997–98). He tied a school record for interception return touchdowns with two, as well as tying the school record with five tackles-for-loss in a game (the 1997 Rose Bowl versus Arizona State).

As a junior in 1998, Andy was a finalist for the Maxwell Football Club's Defensive Player of the Year Award (in addition to the Lombardi Award) and he anchored the nation's top-ranked defense against the run and second-ranked unit in total defense. He was a Lombardi Award finalist, ranking second on the team with 97 tackles, including 13 tackles-for-loss. He clinched the Arizona win with a 20–yard interception return for a touchdown. He had 11 tackles against both Arizona and Iowa. In 1996 he became the first freshman to start every game at linebacker for the Buckeyes and finished second on the team with 85 tackles and paced the team with 23 tackles-for-loss and sacks (12), both school records for a linebacker.

Unfortunately, some Buckeye fans chose to remember Andy as the player who got caught breaking curfew and struggled in the classroom. It still upsets me that *Sports Illustrated* took advantage of his youthful inexperience, and made him the unwitting poster child for all that is allegedly wrong with college athletics. Adding insult to injury, the magazine even made a point of his taking so-called "bunny" courses during the summer to remain eligible. I am not defending the academic choices Andy made during his career at Ohio State, but the mistakes he made are not uncommon for many 18- to 20-year-olds who are still trying to find their place in this world. I'm sure the journalists who chose to attack him have skeletons in their closet from their youth, as we all do. What pains me is that many people interpreted Andy's extreme shyness as being selfish and disrespectful of Ohio State and its traditions, and this is the furthest thing from the truth. Andy, like his hero Chris Spielman, were not vocal players, and chose to let their performance on the football field do the talking. I know for a fact that Andy loves Ohio State, and I hope someday that Ohio State loves him back because he deserves it.

Even though the New England Patriots selected Andy in the first round of the 1999 draft, a serious neck injury ended what was a promising professional career after only two seasons. We will never know what kind of professional player he would have become, but it's difficult to forget his record-tying five tackles for loss against Arizona State in the 1997 Rose Bowl, or the fact that he was one of the hardest hitting defensive players in Buckeye history. Andy loved the game of football, and he will ultimately be remembered as one of the best linebackers in college football history.

Mike Vrabel: The Best College Athlete I Ever Coached

Some people were surprised when New England Patriots linebacker Mike Vrabel caught a touchdown pass in not only one, but two recent Super Bowl games. Not me. I wasn't surprised because Mike Vrabel was the best athlete I encountered during my years as a position coach at Ohio State. I know this is a bold statement, considering the very talented individuals I worked with, but it also is true.

Big (6 feet 4 inches and 261 pounds), fast (he has running back speed), agile and tough, Mike was not only a second-team All-America football player at Walsh Jesuit High School in Stow, Ohio (near Akron), he also lettered in basketball and track, where he finished in third place in the shot put at the Ohio track championships his junior and senior years. He's also extremely intelligent. A pre-med major at Ohio State, Mike was twice selected to the Big

Ten All-Academic team, and is a Pro Football Hall of Fame Scholarship Award winner.

Playing strong-side defensive end for the Buckeyes, Mike used his God-given physical and mental tangibles to his advantage. I'll never forget a play he made during a game against Notre Dame in 1995. Late in the game, Notre Dame had driven the ball down the field and was facing fourth down on our goal line. A score may have given the Fighting Irish the momentum to mount a comeback. We couldn't let that happen. We needed a big play, and Mike would step up to make it just as he had done many times before and continues doing at the professional level. Exploding off the snap, Mike threw aside the opposing tight end like a rag doll on his way to tackling the running back in the backfield. He threw the tight end to the ground with such force that the player's face mask struck before the rest of his body; the way the player's body went limp, I thought Mike had knocked him out or worse. Fortunately, the Notre Dame player was not injured on the play, but Mike's efforts enable us to secure a 29–16 victory.

It should be no surprise that Mike holds Buckeye career records for quarterback sacks (36) and tackles for losses (66). His senior year, Mike earned first-team All-America honors from Walter Camp and the American Football Coaches Association. He also was named first-team All-Big Ten Conference and the Big Ten Defensive Player of the Year for a second-straight season. That year, he recorded 48 tackles (31 solos) and tied for a team lead with nine sacks.

As a junior, Mike started every game at strong-side defensive end and led the conference with a Buckeye season-record

26 stops for losses of 133 yards. He also tied the Big Ten single-season record and broke his own school record with 13 sacks. As sophomore, Mike earned All-Big Ten Conference and Academic Big-Ten first-team honors. He started every game that year and recorded a school-record 12 sacks, a record he would break the following year. Mike made an appearance in every game as a freshman, playing the role of reserve defensive end.

As a linebacker for the New England Patriots, Mike has played a pivotal role in that team's success in winning three Super Bowls over a four-year period between 2001 and 2004. A "play maker," Mike seems to make the right play at the right time. Consider these Super Bowl vignettes:

- In Super Bowl XXXVI, played on February 3, 2002, Mike applied pressure to St. Louis Rams quarterback Kurt Warner, forcing an errant pass that was intercepted by cornerback Ty Law and returned 47 yards for a touchdown, giving the Patriots an early 7–0 lead on their way to an upset victory.

- During the 2003 season, Mike finished second on the team with six tackles (four solo), including a game-high two sacks and also caught a touchdown pass and forced a fumble in the Patriots' 32–29 Super Bowl XXXVIII victory. He gave the Patriots a 29–22 lead with his second career touchdown reception, a one-yard catch from quarterback Tom Brady, with 2:51 left in the game. That play gave Mike the distinction of being the first defensive player since William "The Refrigerator" Perry (Super Bowl XX) to record a touchdown on offense. If that wasn't enough, in that same game, Mike sacked Carolina Panthers quarterback Jake Delhomme for a six-yard loss with a vicious, blindside hit that forced a fumble. The loose ball was recovered by the Patriots and broke a scoreless tie by leading to a first touchdown of the game. Mike also dropped Delhomme for a nine-yard sack on third-and-eight to halt a Panthers drive in the first quarter.

• In 2004, Mike caught three touchdown passes as a tight end in goal line situations, including a two-yard score from quarterback Tom Brady in Super Bowl XXXIX against the Philadelphia Eagles, giving Mike two career touchdowns in Super Bowls—setting a new record for defensive players on offense—and the Patriots a 14–7 lead. In addition, he collected four tackles (two solo), including a sack in the Patriots' 24–21 victory over the Eagles. Mike also sacked Eagles quarterback Donovan McNabb for a 16-yard loss.

There's not much more I can say about this special individual, except that at the writing of this book he was preparing to enter his tenth year in the NFL. At age 30, I believe Mike is only beginning to tap his potential on and off the field. By the way, Mike returned to Ohio State during off-seasons to complete his college degree.

The special athletes I just discussed continue making their mark on the gridiron and in the communities where they play. There is one other athlete, however, I did not include in this chapter and whom I also recruited to play for Ohio State. This athlete's story is so unique and so compelling that I felt it deserved its own chapter. This athlete is none other than Heisman Trophy winner Eddie George.

Conley's Recruiting Commandments

VIII. Be able to look yourself in the mirror.

At the end of the day, a recruiter knows he's done well if he was honest and forthright with recruits. There's nothing more rewarding than knowing you put in a hard day's work and you did it the right way.

One of my most rewarding recruiting efforts was getting a commitment from Florida superstar Chris Gamble. Even though recruiters from other universities used what I believe are questionable tactics, we won the battle by telling the truth and being direct with Chris and his family. (You can read more about Chris in chapter 9.)

That's Eddie and me posing with his Heisman Trophy.

"The Flying Elvises," including (from left to right): Lovie
Smith, Bill Young, Joe Hollis, Fred Pagac, Tim Spencer, Eddie,
Head Coach John Cooper, Walt Harris, Me, Larry Petroff, Mike
Jacobs (and kneeling) Chuck Stobart and Dave Kennedy.

8

Eddie George

Rising from Obscurity to the Heisman Trophy and Super Bowl

The first time I heard the name Eddie George was when one of our student athletic trainers mentioned it in passing at practice in late September 1991. The trainer, Dan Osman, said George was a running back at his high school alma mater, Fork Union Military Academy in Virginia, and was having an exceptional senior year.

My initial thought was, "Fork what?" My next thought was, "Yeah, right. If this Eddie George is that good, why haven't we heard about him before now from either his high school coach or one of the plethora of recruiting services and publications that seem to be popular these days?"

Then I thought, quite cynically, "If I had a dollar for every parent or friend of a player that believed their son or buddy could play at Ohio State, I wouldn't have to coach for a living."

Besides, we already had one of the country's best young running backs and future NFL star, a freshman by the name of Robert Smith, and a cadre of other talented backs on our roster. Actually, we were steep in running backs at that juncture, but I didn't want to be rude. Besides, Osman was persistent about the talent possessed by this Eddie George. So, I instructed Osman to come to my office the following day with the name and phone number of the Fork Union head coach. I have to admit now that I made this suggestion half thinking Osman would forget about it, meaning I could get back to the pressing business of winning football games and tracking down legitimate recruits from around the country. You see, at the time, prep schools such as Fork Union weren't being heavily recruited and not very well-respected as many athletes attending those schools were doing so for reasons that had nothing to do with football. Many of these young men had personal, familial, social or academic issues in their backgrounds. Besides, there were just too many good student-athletes from better-known high schools or even junior colleges to consider by programs such as Ohio State.

Well, the next day like clockwork Osman called my bluff and was waiting for me outside my office at 8 A.M. with a phone number for Fork Union head coach John Shuman. I could have thrown the note away and got onto the business at hand, but something told me to at least make the phone call to a military academy I knew nothing about. So, the following day, I called Coach Shuman and had a conversation something like this:

"Is this Coach John Shuman?"

"Yes, sir," said the raspy voice on the other end, his military background resonating through the line.

"Hello, this is Coach Bill Conley with the Ohio State Buckeyes," I said.

"Yes, sir. How may I help you, sir?" said Shuman.

"Do you have a running back by the name of Eddie George?" I asked.

"Yes, sir," he said.

"Is he good?" I continued.

"Yes, sir," he responded once again without an explanation.

"May I get some film of him?" I inquired further.

"Yes, sir," he said.

"May I ask another question?" I continued.

"Yes, sir," Shuman said.

"Is he being recruited by anyone else at this time?"

"Yes, sir. The University of Louisville," he said.

"Thank you," I said before hanging up.

"Thank you, sir," he said before hanging up.

The conversation raised more questions in my mind. I don't know if it was the matter-of-fact tone in Coach Shuman's voice, or the fact that no other "big-time" Division I school was even looking at this kid. I just couldn't shake some misgivings I had about this Eddie George. I remember thinking, "Either this kid is truly a diamond in the rough, or he just isn't good enough to cut it at a school like Ohio State and a town like Columbus, Ohio, where fans and the media have high expectations and can be unforgiving at times."

Because we were in mid-season, and I was working 16- to 18-hour days, I honestly did not give Eddie George another thought until a tape arrived a week later. When I received it, I prepared myself mentally to watch 10 plays and write a polite note back to Coach Shuman, essentially stating, "Thanks but no thanks. Please extend our warmest regards to Eddie, and best wishes as he pursues other endeavors." I even had a pen and note card on my desk by the projector to make things easier for me.

Boy, was I in for a surprise! The images on the tape were grainy and sometimes out of focus, but I remember immediately being impressed with the size, speed and power of this young man . . . he was too good to be true for a high school senior. Eddie seemed to be every bit of the 6 feet 3 inches and 215 pounds they had him listed at in the program. And during that particular game, he completely dominated offensive play. The first play from scrimmage, he busted up the middle, ran over a linebacker and picked up eight yards. The second play, he went off tackle to the right, bulled over several defenders and ran 40 yards for a touchdown. He would score two more touchdowns before halftime and two others in the second half. A note from Coach Shuman included with the tape stated that Eddie was in the process of breaking most of Fork Union's single-season rushing records.

Maybe you've already guessed my reaction, but I began questioning the level of competition Eddie was facing and whether he could compete in the Big Ten. Remember, it was my job to recruit the best of the best, meaning second best didn't cut it. Also, another bad rap on prep schools back then was that the level of competition was not even close to what you see with regular high school programs. Additionally, Eddie was playing prep school football in Virginia; this wasn't Texas, California, Florida, Pennsylvania or Ohio, all of which are renown for the quality of high school competition.

"This must be a fluke," I said to myself.

So, I called Coach Shuman once again, and after another brief, dispassionate conversation arranged to receive another tape. Again, I went about the business at hand until the tape arrived a week later. To my surprise, Eddie performed even better in the second tape, so I decided to invite him for an "official" recruiting visit. But before I extended the offer, I made sure to inquire once again whether any other large, Division I schools were recruiting Eddie. Again, I was told, "No, just Louisville."

It was at this point I told head coach John Cooper about Eddie George from Fork Union Military Academy in Virginia. Not surprisingly, John expressed the same reservations I had, so I urged him to watch the tapes. After doing so, he eagerly supported my decision to arrange the visit, which was scheduled for the second week in December that year.

Why is the time frame of the visit so important? Well, it proves that our idea of keeping this diamond in the rough a secret was too good to be true. While confirming with Coach Shuman details of Eddie's visit a few weeks ahead of time, I learned that Notre Dame and our archrival, Michigan, had jumped into the recruiting fray. They obviously heard that we were recruiting Eddie. Yes, in college football as in politics and business there is very little that remains a secret. "Damnit," I thought, learning that Eddie had scheduled visits at those schools in January. My heart sank because Eddie's status as a legitimate, Division I recruit was now confirmed. I tried to remain optimistic about our chances of landing him and hoped that our early interest would pay dividends.

I will never forget the first time I met Eddie George in person, as he arrived at the gate at Port Columbus International Airport. Dressed in his gray and blue military uniform, he possessed the physical presence of the prototypical, big and physical Division I running back. Even more impressive was the fact that he was articulate, intelligent and polite. He also projected an aura of leadership about him I've only seen in a handful of high school athletes. After so many years in coaching and working with some great student-athletes—Chris Spielman and Cris Carter, to name a couple—I thought I couldn't be this easily impressed, but I was with Eddie George. Something told me immediately that this young man was special and that we had to convince him that it was his destiny to become a Buckeye.

I'll also never forget the moment I met Eddie's mother, Donna, a flight attendant and single mother, who sent her only son to a military prep school to get him away from the temptations and potential trouble on the streets of inner-city Philadelphia. She wanted her son to have opportunities only a solid education could bring, and it seemed that football was second on her mind as she literally drilled our coaching staff and other university officials with questions, the answers of which she dutifully logged in a large phonebook-sized notebook she carried everywhere with her. To this day, I've never been asked so many questions by a parent during a 48-hour official campus visit.

I really thought the visit was going well, but doubts still lingered. During a brief coaches' meeting the morning before Eddie was scheduled to fly home, I remember telling Coach Cooper that I believed we had, at best, a 20 percent chance of landing this recruit. I remember consoling myself with the knowledge that we still had a number of outstanding running backs already in the program, and that the loss of one athlete wouldn't injure a tradition-steeped program like Ohio State. But deep down I wanted this young man to be a Buckeye; I continued to have this feeling at my core that he was something very special and had positive qualities that transcended the gridiron. To my relief, my fears proved unwarranted as I walked with Eddie and his mother through the airport to catch their plane home. As we reached the gate and I prepared to say goodbye, Eddie turned to me, put his hand on my shoulder and said he wanted to "commit" to play for Ohio State. I felt as if I had won the lottery, I was so relieved, excited and frightened at once. Then reality sank in and I made sure to explain to Eddie that, if he was committing to us, he had to cancel planned visits to Notre Dame and Michigan. I had to make sure this situation wasn't too good to be true, and that he knew what he was saying to me. Without hesitation, he stood tall and looked me straight in the eyes and told me that he understood completely. He said this was his final decision, reiterating that he wanted to attend Ohio State, be a Buckeye and earn a college degree. I have to admit now that I still had some doubts. I guess this comes from so many years of working with teenagers and knowing how fickle the minds of 17- and 18-year-olds can be. I mean we've had recruits change their minds and turn down scholarship offers because of a variety of reasons, including distance from home, or the influence of a high school coach or girlfriend.

But with regards to Eddie, the rest is history, as they say. He stayed true to his word, and would not only become a Buckeye but go on to become one of the greatest running backs in the school's history and win the Heisman Trophy his senior year. He also would become a "franchise" running back with the Houston Oilers and then the Tennessee Titans of the National Football League. He would be named the 1996 NFL

Rookie of the Year. He would lead the Titans to a berth in Super Bowl XXXIV against the St. Louis Rams. St. Louis won the game 23–16, after the Titans fell one yard short of scoring a touchdown—and possibly tying the score—on the final play from scrimmage in the fourth quarter.

Of all the fond memories I have of Eddie as a player, the following one stands out as a testament to the mettle of the man: Buckeye and college football fans may remember a game against Illinois during Eddie's freshman year in 1992, when he fumbled and lost the ball on not one but two key scoring drives inside the Illinois 10–yard line. We wound up losing the game, and as a coaching staff we questioned whether this young man with so much raw, physical talent could elevate the mental part of his play to be successful in the Big Ten. Unfortunately, I and every other college coach I know have seen many high school stars that fail to make it at the next level, especially in Division I football. In Eddie's case, he not only proved us wrong, but he also made us eat our doubts. The following two seasons, Eddie committed himself to never letting his team down again. And going into his senior season, he was touted by the national media as one of the top returning running backs. While the team was doing its rigorous off-season workouts, Eddie did twice that and enhanced his already awesome, God-given physical abilities. At the start of the 1995 season, Eddie was 6 feet 3 inches, 230 pounds. Making him even more impressive is the fact that he had less than 5 percent body fat, meaning he was ripped like no other athlete I've ever seen or believe I'll ever see. He also made a personal commitment to be "fumble free" the rest of his career as a Buckeye, and he kept that commitment. Maybe it was irony or fate, but it was against

Illinois his senior year in 1995 when Eddie shattered Ohio State's single-game rushing record by gaining 314 yards on 36 carries and scoring two touchdowns to lead the Buckeyes to an impressive 41–3 victory on one of the coldest days I can remember at Ohio Stadium.

Eddie was a long shot for the Heisman Trophy when the 1995 season began, even though he was widely recognized as one of the nation's top running backs. By the time the season ended, there was very little doubt who had truly earned the honor as the nation's most valuable player for his team. Eddie beat out runner-up Tommy Frazier of Nebraska and third-place finisher Troy Davis of Iowa State for the much-coveted trophy. Eddie became the sixth Heisman Trophy recipient in Ohio State history and etched his name into the university's record book by rushing for a school-record 1,927 yards and 24 touchdowns. Included in that yardage total were three 200-yard games, including the storied Illinois game. The other 200-yard games were against Washington (219 yards, and the first of 12 consecutive, 100-yard games) and Notre Dame (207 yards).

Eddie ended the 1995 campaign leading the country in scoring with an average of 12.1 points per game. He also finished fourth in all-purpose running (185.4) and fifth in rushing (152.1). His other honors that year included the Doak Walker Award, the Maxwell Award, the Walter Camp Player of the Year Award, and Big Ten MVP. He also was a team co-captain.

Eddie finished his career with the Buckeyes as the second-leading rusher in Ohio State history with 3,668 yards.

Although facts and statistics are intriguing, they don't tell the whole story. Permit me to share stories surrounding Eddie's receiving of the Heisman Trophy and the signing of his professional contract. Concerning the former event, it is customary for the head coach to travel with the Heisman candidate to the New York Athletic Club for the official announcement, so Coach Cooper was with Eddie when he was announced as the 1995 winner. Because the Heisman is awarded during recruiting season, the rest of the coaching staff used the event as an opportunity to showcase Ohio State to a group of recruits. We packed recruits, their parents or guardians, as well as several current player-hosts into a local sports restaurant and watched the ceremony unfold on big-screen televisions. I probably do not have to mention the fact that Eddie's accomplishments helped sway the decisions of a number of recruits that particular evening, as that year we landed a recruiting class considered No. 1 in the nation by most media and recruiting outlets. That year alone, we signed Andy Katzenmoyer, David Boston, Gary Berry, Jr., Joe Germaine, Ahmed Plummer, Michael Wiley and Nick Goings. All of these players became outstanding players for the Buckeyes, and several continue to play professional football today.

It was customary for the New York Athletic Club to hold a black-tie dinner the Monday after the Saturday award presentation. Coach Cooper called me Monday morning and said he wanted the entire coaching staff to come to the dinner. All I remember saying is: "You want us where? You want us when? And you want us wearing what?"

Neither I nor any of the other coaches owned a tuxedo at that time, so we immediately rushed to O.P. Gallo, a tux shop in downtown Columbus, and rented matching black tuxedos. We decided to wear them on the plane to save time, as we'd have only enough time to travel directly to the dinner from the airport. What a sight it must have been to see eight rather large, athletically built men in black tuxedos running through airports in Columbus and then Philadelphia, where we had a brief layover before flying into LaGuardia. You know how certain situations take on a life of their own? Well, as we boarded the plane in Philadelphia, a flight attendant quipped that we looked like a singing group. Well, that's all it took for assistant coach Fred Pagac to tell her that we were in fact the Flying Elvises, Columbus, Ohio Chapter. He then pointed at me, telling her I was the "head Elvis." The jibe seemed quite apropos because I've been given that tag before by my friends. Well, wouldn't you know it that as we began to taxi on the runway in Philadelphia, the pilot got on the intercom to say, "Please enjoy your flight to New York City. And by the way, I'd like to extend warm wishes to the Flying Elvises from Columbus, Ohio. Welcome aboard, gentlemen," he said, doing a fairly convincing Elvis impersonation. To make a long story short, we arrived at the dinner just in time to see Eddie honored once again. I cannot describe how I felt that night watching this young man whom I had met only four years prior. All I can say is that I was misty eyed as an overwhelming sense of pride, admiration and accomplishment came over me. The feelings fortified a deep affinity I have for this special athlete, a man I still consider a friend today. Eddie had literally risen from obscurity to national celebrity, and would be a first-round pick in the 1996 NFL draft.

The day Eddie signed with the Houston Oilers (who became the Tennessee Titans that year) was just as special, but tarnished by tragedy. You see, Eddie desperately wanted his mother to fly to Houston for the signing. To do so, Donna George had to beg and barter to get her flight schedule changed. She was able to make the necessary arrangements to be with her only child on this special occasion and celebrate all they had accomplished together. However, the day—July 17, 1996— is always remembered with much sadness by many, as the flight Donna George was supposed to work—Flight 800 out of New York to Paris—crashed into the Atlantic Ocean near Moriches Inlet shortly after lifting off from Kennedy International Airport, killing all 229 people aboard. Luck or fate saved Donna George that day, but an event like this serves as a poignant reminder that life is fleeting.

Another positive sidebar of the Eddie George saga is the fact that John Shuman, his prep school coach, and Mickey Sullivan, Fork Union's athletic director, remain very good friends of mine and of The Ohio State University to this day. It seems Eddie opened a pipeline between the prep school and the university, as several other top Fork Union student-athletes have continued their careers at Ohio State, including tight end Ricky Dudley. The 6 feet 8 inch Dudley played football and basketball at Ohio State, and parlayed that into a successful career as a tight end with the Oakland Raiders. To their credit, Shuman and Sullivan continued to volunteer to work youth camps and combines for many years after Eddie and others left the university, demonstrating the power of human connections.

Finally, I'd be remiss if I didn't also point out that Eddie stayed true to the most important promise he made to his mother even before committing to play football at Ohio State, and that was to earn a college degree. Admirably, Eddie returned to campus during the NFL off-season to continue his studies toward a bachelor's degree in landscape architecture— one of Ohio State's most difficult and demanding majors. Though Eddie made headlines many times as a collegiate and professional football player, I don't think I was ever so proud as I was on a day in June 2001, when Eddie and thousands of other Ohio State graduates filed into Ohio Stadium to be awarded their diplomas. Some would argue it was Eddie's finest moment in that arena, and I would not disagree.

The bottom line is that our sport, our universities and our nation need more student-athletes like Eddie George. He epitomizes the better side of that sometimes dysfunctional relationship between athletics and academics.

Conley's Recruiting Commandments

IX. Home visits: Have your proverbial gun loaded.

The first home visit is critical to success. Make sure you've done your homework, as this will be the best shot at getting an "official" visit from a recruit. Be organized, complete, unassuming and most importantly, be a good listener.

I always took pride in being in the home of my top recuits the first day such visits were allowed by the NCAA. This assertiveness, I believe, showed the recruits they were indeed a high priority to the program.

Sideline adjustments during the Nokia Sugar Bowl versus Florida State, played on January 1, 1998. The Buckeyes lost that game 34-14.

The Road to Tempe

Jim Tressel and the 2002 National Championship Team

As Miami Hurricane quarterback Ken Dorsey's fourth-down pass during a second overtime period bounced to the turf incomplete, the world seemed to stand still. A moment that felt like an eternity, but what was in reality a second or two changed as I watched our players and fans swarm the field at Sun Devil Stadium. In the wee hours of January 3, 2003, we had won the national championship, beating the much-heralded and feared Miami Hurricanes in the process. As one of the coaches in the press box, in those few seconds after that last play, I along with assistant coaches Joe Daniels, Mark Dantonio and Mel Tucker, scanned the field for penalty flags to make sure that results of the play stood. Seeing none, we momentarily stared at one another as if to ask, "Is this really true?" Realizing it was true, we erupted in shouts as we began congratulating one another in a flurry of "high-fives" and pats on the back. We were 14–0 and now the National Champions of Division I college football. The words "undefeated" give me goose bumps to this very day. After our short-lived celebration in the press box, we made our way to the elevator to go join the team and the rest of the coaching staff. It seemed like the elevator stopped a dozen times on the way down, and that only fueled our excitement about what awaited us on the field and in the locker room. On one stop, a well-known senator from the state of Florida got on and started complaining rather loudly about the officiating. In a rare moment of boastfulness, Mark Dantonio retorted that the Buckeyes simply dominated the Hurricanes physically from beginning to end and were simply the better team that evening. He said it just loud enough for the politician to turn his head and give us an absolutely evil stare, which only caused all of us to begin laughing uncontrollably as the senator made a rather hurried exit at the next floor.

Finally reaching the ground floor from the press box at Sun Devil Stadium, we jumped into an awaiting golf cart to get to the on-field awards ceremony. Already gathered at the 50–yard line was most of the team and the families and friends of players and coaches alike. I even saw Columbus mayor Michael Coleman, who had joined the celebration. The atmosphere was simply electric, as much of the overwhelming Buckeye contingent that made the trip to Arizona refused to leave the stadium and launched into an impromptu party. I remember my ears ringing from the noise and the positive energy that surrounded our team.

After the awards ceremony, the entire Buckeye entourage made its way to the end zone where the Ohio State Marching

Band was seated. There, we continued our custom of singing *Carmen Ohio,* which is the Ohio State Alma Mater. Though this experience was always very emotional after victories, it was even more powerful that day. We were singing not only for ourselves, but for the entire university and the whole state of Ohio. I thought to myself once again: "We are the national champions."

As the song concluded, we quickly made our way to the locker room, where players and coaches continued to celebrate with one another. I remember feeling fortunate that I was able to bring along my own sons, Bill and Craig, to experience the locker room atmosphere. It was a special moment for me as a coach and as a father because I rarely had such an opportunity with my sons. As a football coach, particularly one at the Division I college level, you spend so much time with other people's children that your own family suffers. For me, the greatest part of this incredible night was being able to share it with my boys.

It seemed like hours after the game before the buses were ready to head back to Fairmont Princess Resort. The hour was definitely late, but as the convoy left Sun Devil Stadium, Ohio State fans lined the road to cheer for the team. Back at the resort, I was finally able to take time for quiet reflection on what we had just accomplished, and what the reasons were that this particular team stood out from so many more than I had been a part of during my tenure at Ohio State.

The 2002 Season

Coach Jim Tressel was preparing to coach his second full season at Ohio State after taking over following the firing of John Cooper. During our first season under Jim in 2001, the Buckeyes went a respectful 7–5, but most importantly, we beat Michigan in Ann Arbor, 26–20. That win in itself was significant because it gave the Buckeye faithful something to believe in again.

The 2002 campaign was crucial for the second-year head coach. Jim's philosophy, routine, staff and system now had been in place for one year, and it was time to see if it would fly. Even so, a majority of the top-notched talent on that team—especially the starters—was recruited during the John Cooper years. It would be interesting to see how everything would mesh as we prepared to open the season against Texas Tech.

Three of us on the coaching staff, including Jim Heacock, Tim Spencer and myself, had been part of Cooper's staff. Each of us bought into Jim's philosophy even though we found him to be much more aloof than Cooper. I know Tim and I, two former Ohio State players, felt this way and never really felt as much a part of the "Jim Tressel Circle" as the rest of the staff did. It was obvious that the connections he brought from his successful tenure at Youngstown State University held a higher priority. Please don't get me wrong—I am not sour about the opportunity I was given to continue coaching at Ohio State, but I think it's important to understand the team dynamic of the time. I am well aware that in coaching, as well as other walks of life, it's not uncommon for a new leader to surround himself with trusted and loyal assistants. Despite an apparent caste system within the staff, each and every coach gave the proverbial 110 percent to the program and the players. The bottom line is that we were all professionals and that is the only way to conduct business in my book. Personally, I sold Jim Tressel and Ohio State University to parents, recruits, coaches and alumni as hard as I sold Earle Bruce and John Cooper. From an external view, everything was as it always had been from my perspective. No one coach has all the answers, no one is all saint or all sinner, and there's a lot of ways to "skin a cat." That year, that time, and for 14 games, we were all "one" team.

As practice concluded in the spring of 2002 and the players finalized the third academic quarter of the school year, the focus on the upcoming season intensified. It was during player meetings at that time that Jim Tressel made a masterful motivational move. He passed out to the juniors and seniors on the team a copy of a book entitled *Expanding Your Horizons.* The book was written by Dr. Donald Steinberg and focuses on the 1942 Ohio State national championship team coached by the legendary Paul Brown. As a matter of fact, each chapter in the book is about a specific player. The personal stories of Buckeye greats such as Les Horvath, Dante Lavelli, Bob Shaw, Gene Fekete, Bill Willis, Bill Hackett, Jack Dugger and Chuck Csuri, as well as Steinberg, are discussed on and off the gridiron, and following their college playing days.

Coach Tressel told each junior and senior that during summer practices they were required to give a report to the rest of the team on an assigned chapter. This was a first for Ohio State, and something I consider a brilliant move today. (By the way, the entire coaching staff also was assigned a chapter to report on.) As each of us began reading, it became crystal clear why Jim chose this particular book. The players would learn several valuable life lessons as well as build a stronger bridge to something that can be intangible for some players, and that's Buckeye Tradition. Something that struck me about the 1942 team was how this particular group was not only successful in football, but also in their professional and personal lives. Members of that team went on to become prominent scientists, physicians, coaches, administrators and business executives. Following the 1942 season, a majority of those players went off to serve during World War II; some became war heroes. Chuck Csuri, for example, was awarded the Bronze Star for single-handedly saving his battalion from German forces near Bastogne, France. Csuri, a Buckeye offensive lineman, was selected to captain the 1943 team, but felt a stronger calling to serve his country. Csuri typified many of the young men on that national championship team. Another trait of the 1942 team was how a group of small, relatively obscure athletes could pull together to achieve the ultimate prize of college football. I find it ironic that 60 years later a team that was not even picked to win the Big Ten would achieve the same reward.

The motivational value of the book reports became vividly apparent as each player faced his peers each evening after summer two-a-day practices. The underlining message that each player was beginning to understand was that he was merely a small part of a massive tradition. They were no longer better or worse than those who came before them, but they had an opportunity to do something special to strengthen Ohio State tradition. To fully connect our current players to the past, Jim scheduled Csuri and Steinberg to speak with our team that season. Even though many of the members of the 1942 team were no longer alive, you could somehow feel their presence as we began our march to Tempe.

Another unique thing would happen each August evening. After the team meetings and book reports, and before the guys left the auditorium of the Fawcett Center, senior linebacker Cie Grant would stand up, get up on stage and lead the team in singing *Carmen Ohio*. This would continue each night during the season, and the players would make their way to the marching band in the South Stands at Ohio Stadium after home games to continue this new, old tradition. Cie Grant, whose singing talents matched his physical skills on the football field, would become a key leader on that team.

The 2002 season kicked off with an impressive, 45–21 win over Texas Tech. Subsequent and substantial victories over Kent State and Washington State were just the start we needed. Senior co-captains Michael Doss and Donnie Nickey were showing great leadership. Even though most of the early season debate centered on two-way player Chris Gamble and freshman-phenomenon Maurice Clarett, it was the concept of "team" that our seniors extolled that impressed all of us involved with the program.

The commitment and resolve of our senior class would reveal itself throughout the season during close victories against Cincinnati, Northwestern, Wisconsin, Penn State and Purdue. It showed in our overtime victory over Illinois and was much apparent in our victory of archrival Michigan to complete the undefeated string and finish the regular season 13–0. Five of the aforementioned nine wins were by a touchdown or less. Fans remember the big plays, such as Chris Gamble's interception versus Cincinnati, Greg Krenzel's touchdown pass to Michael Jenkins at Purdue, or Maurice Hall's touchdown on an option play at the closed end of the Horseshoe against Michigan. However, the great plays made by players such as Will Smith, Tim Anderson, Matt Wilhelm, Dustin Fox, Ben Hartsock, Darrion Scott, Robert Reynolds, Alex Stepanovich and the other Buckeyes already mentioned became commonplace that season. The consistency of place kicker Mike Nugent, punter Andy Groom and long-snapper Kyle Andrews were equally impressive. The most apparent point about this team was how these athletes, who were from all parts of our country, came together to find a way to win. It was like each person was on a mission not to let their teammates down, no matter what obstacle or challenge they faced. They simply overcame adversity at all levels during the fall of 2002. It was like they were destined to repeat the achievement of the Buckeyes who came 60 years before them, and they would not be denied their destiny.

As mentioned, another remarkable characteristic about the 2002 Buckeyes is how the team fought through adversity time and again. Some of the challenges they faced could tear an ordinary team apart, but this was no ordinary team. Most of the distractions that season were caused by freshman running back Maurice Clarett, whom I will discuss later in this chapter. The bottom line with Maurice is that although he demonstrated remarkable abilities on the field, he showed extreme selfishness and immaturity off the field. The team, which could have allowed Maurice's antics to derail their performance, seemed to pay little attention to him and gave it very little concern. They remained focused and true to their mission of winning each and every game, and that speaks volumes about the character of this group of young men.

Following our 14–9 victory over Michigan in Columbus, the team and coaches made plans to travel to Tempe, Arizona, to face the Miami Hurricanes in the Tostitos Fiesta Bowl for the title of national champion. The only other times Ohio State had faced Miami was in the 1977 season opener, which the Buckeyes won 10–0, and the 1999 Kick-Off Classic, which we lost 23–12. I was, however, very familiar with many of the Hurricane players and coaches because I had been recruiting in Florida for many, many years. I had also been in many of the schools and homes of the players while trying to lure them to Ohio State. Miami was very skilled with great team speed, but they would soon find out that the 2002 Buckeyes had a fair amount of skill, and much more speed than Big Ten teams are usually given credit for having.

The Miami Hurricanes were the defending national champions, and the media gave Ohio State very little chance of winning. It seemed like every time we picked up a newspaper or watched the television it wasn't going to be a question of whether Miami was going to win, but by how many points they would win. The game was supposed to be so lopsided that the Buckeyes could save themselves much embarrassment if they did not play. The negative press, along with a flier we intercepted advertising a post-game Miami victory celebration, provided some extra incentive to the players. To their credit, most of the players continued to show a polite, respectful face in public, but we knew deep down they were boiling over. They had something to prove to the football world, the media, the fans and most importantly to themselves. The watching and waiting only made this passion burn hotter.

Jim allowed the players to establish a curfew during the pre-game practice sessions in Tempe. This astonished and confused many on the coaching staff who were not certain if these young men could make and manage such a mature decision. Not only did they set reasonable curfew hours, they set earlier times than what the coaches would have established and they made sure no player was violating the "team" rules. Team leaders from every position would not allow their teammates to go to bed each night without watching more film of Miami. They dissected the Hurricanes completely, uncovering strengths, weaknesses and hidden tendencies that would give them an edge on the field.

As game day approached, the staff and players became more and more confident. Great leadership by the players resulted in great practice sessions. Every single player on our traveling team, including red-shirted and second team players, seemed to be focused on something that transcended themselves. Our scout team players forced our starters to get better and better as preparations intensified heading to the January 3 game. As coaches, we did not know if we'd win, but what we did know was that the Buckeyes would give the Hurricanes one hell of a fight. We could see that in the eyes of each and every player, and it was a marvelous thing.

The only sound made during the bus ride to Sun Devil Stadium on game day was the throaty growl of the diesel engines. The players, many of whom listened to personal radios and CD players, were strangely quiet and subdued. Many reviewed paperwork, going over assignments for the game and making one last review of Miami scouting reports. As we pulled into the stadium parking lot, the noise outside the bus intensified as Buckeye fans swarmed the vehicle. One fan lost his footing trying to run alongside the bus and fell flat on his face on the sidewalk. That had to have hurt, but the fan quickly got up and continued his efforts, now sporting some bloody scrapes on his face and hands. Somehow, I don't think this particular fan really felt those injuries until the next day, but I could be wrong. Most of the players seemed to take this incident in stride, shrugging it off as if to say, "This is big-time college football."

Stopping outside of the team entrance area, the noise became deafening as players filed into the locker room through a gauntlet of Scarlet and Gray fanatics. Yes, this sort of activity does motivate you as a player and coach, as you can feel the support and pride of the Buckeye faithful. It served to reinforce what was our primary mission . . . to win. After so many years in coaching, I never really concentrated on the simple act of changing into my coaching attire. That day in Arizona, however, my mind was aware of each and every movement I was making. After getting dressed, I walked onto the field to take in the atmosphere. That season, I usually went out earlier than some of the other coaches because I was in charge of specialty players (kickers, punters, long snappers), along with tight ends. As I walked toward midfield, I could feel the warmth of the setting Arizona sun. Even though it was January, the intensity of the sun there is still very powerful, especially for those of us from Ohio who hadn't really seen the sun since winter set in. Standing at midfield, the magnitude of this event struck me like a semi truck. This was it. This is what I'd worked my whole life for . . . a chance to be part of the college football national championship as a coach. Even though I had been a player for the Buckeyes in 1968, the last time Ohio State won a national championship, I did not play in that game. It was now January 3, 2003, and I felt a sense of pride that I had played a role in getting this team to this position. It was as if the many hours and many years of coaching, traveling and recruiting had all come together. I also knew that, win or lose, I truly believed I had served my alma mater well, and the sense of gratification I felt that day still sticks with me. I especially appreciated the team effort that got us here, and I am speaking from a coach's perspective. My contributions were no more important than any other coach on the staff. We all worked long hours, we all were committed to these young men, and we all had made personal sacrifices to get this team to this point.

As my eyes scanned Sun Devil Stadium, I noticed a large imbalance in the colors worn by fans who were already filing in and taking their seats. The sea of Scarlet and Gray seemed to consume the amount of green and orange worn by Miami fans. Somewhat facetiously, I thought to myself, "Are we playing at Ohio Stadium?" The contrast was that severe and only grew in intensity as our specialists took the field for pre-game preparations. "We're playing before a home crowd," I thought to myself. "This is utterly amazing." I almost felt sorry for Hurricane fans . . . well, not really!

I learned weeks after the game how such a disparity occurred. It seems that legions of Ohio State alumni living in South Florida joined the Miami Hurricanes booster club to buy tickets. By the time the athletic department at Miami realized what was happening, it was too late. You gotta love Buckeye ingenuity!

The Buckeyes beat the Hurricanes 31–24 in a four-and-one-half hour, double overtime street brawl. Some football pundits continue to call it the "Greatest College Football Game Ever Played," and they won't get any disagreement from me. Bolstering this claim is the fact that it became an instant ESPN Classic and is replayed to this day. I compare the game to a prize fight because it included all the characteristics of a championship heavyweight bout. You had two of the best big-time football programs squaring off and giving one another their best shots. The game was a highlight reel of big plays made at critical times for both teams. You had the drama of the high-scoring, dynamic Miami offense going toe-to-toe with one of the stingiest, battle-proven defenses that year. You had the much-underrated, but fundamentally sound and opportunistic Ohio State offense going against a quick and hard-hitting Miami defense. Both teams had strong kicking games, although I and other game experts gave Ohio State the edge in this category. The night was a big-play buffet accented by big hits, big returns and big kicks.

As fate would have it, this great game went into overtime not once but twice. Miami quarterback Ken Dorsey and his teammates had one last chance to keep the Hurricanes alive, but they had to convert on a fourth down inside the Ohio State two-yard line. As I mentioned earlier in this chapter, his pass fell incomplete. What I didn't mention was the fact that the Buckeye who forced the pass by blitzing off the edge was senior linebacker Cie Grant. Yes, the same Cie Grant who stood up in front of his teammates each night during August training and personally lead the team in singing *Carmen Ohio*. You can push this off to coincidence, or you could attribute it to fate completing the story. All I can say is that it seemed very fitting that this special young man who helped set a tone for this team early on and was able to close the deal and win a national championship. It doesn't get any sweeter than that!

I could write a separate book about the 2002 season alone, but I believe someone beat me to that punch. And why not? The various dynamics of that team, from the off-season and preseason efforts of coaches and players alike, the individual performances, to the drama caused by Maurice Clarett during the undefeated march are all compelling. I've shared with you a few locker room perspectives, and I'd like to expand on that concept by looking at three players who made their marks, respectively, on that special team. These players are flanker/cornerback

Chris Gamble, who was a sophomore that year, place kicker Mike Nugent and Clarett, the sensational-yet-controversial freshman running back. I want to say for the record that while I recruited Gamble and Nugent, I was not involved in the effort to recruit Clarett. The reason I will focus on these three players is because I seem to get more questions about them than anybody else.

Chris Gamble: Redefining the Word "Slash"

I attended a spring practice at Dillard High School in Ft. Lauderdale, Florida, in the spring of 1999. I didn't go there because I had a particular player on my recruiting list. I went because I had been recruiting South Florida for over a decade, and Dillard head coach Joe Redmond is a longtime acquaintance. Besides, the program he had built at Dillard was perennially rich with potential Division I athletes. Redmond and I have known one another since the mid-1970s, when he was head coach at Central State University in Wilberforce, Ohio.

That day, there were at least six other college recruiters on the sidelines watching practice. On one play, a junior receiver by the name of Chris Gamble ran a fade route. He was wide open by the time the quarterback threw the ball, which got away from him and sailed toward the sideline heading for a drainage ditch four feet deep, just 10 feet from the out-of-bounds area. Either Gamble did not realize he was close to the ditch, or didn't care as he sprinted to get beneath the ball. Gamble and the ball reached the drainage ditch at the same time, as he dove trying to make a catch. Both Gamble and the ball disappeared, and stunned silence overcame the practice field. I thought, "Oh, my God, this kid is either severely injured or worse." The look on another recruiter's face from the University of Tennessee told me he was thinking the same thing. We both held our breath.

After what seemed like an eternity, everyone on the field ran toward the ditch. "That kid must have broken a leg," the Tennessee recruiter gasped as we ran. Suddenly, a hand rose from the ditch, clutching the football. The hand was followed by the rest of Gamble, who smiled as he crawled out of the ditch and trotted back to practice. For me, it was another "holy shit" moment, similar to one I experienced almost two decades prior when Cris Carter jumped flat-footed from the ground to a loading dock platform at Middletown High School. "That is no ordinary human being," I remember saying to the gentleman from Tennessee, who also stood there with a dumbfounded look on his face. After that play, Chris Gamble was on the radar of the Ohio State Buckeyes.

It is not uncommon for Dillard High School to produce up to 10 Division I-caliber players a year. The challenge therein is that students from Dillard, which is located in an economically depressed section of Ft. Lauderdale, often struggle in the classroom. Also, because of strong alumni organizations in that area, the best student-athletes tended to go to Auburn University or Michigan State. (For example, former Michigan State running back Lorenzo White graduated from Dillard, and then returned there as an assistant coach following his playing days.) Prior to Chris, the only student-athlete from Dillard I recruited to come to Ohio State was Thomas Mathews, a safety/linebacker, who became a solid special-teams player for the Buckeyes earlier this decade and who would also be part of the national championship team. His father, Thomas Sr., was also an assistant coach at Dillard.

Because it was the spring before Gamble's junior year, all I could do was send a letter expressing our interest in him and keep an eye on his performance. Gamble had a solid junior season, and if he repeated his performance his senior year, we decided we would invite him to make an official visit to Ohio State. His senior season, Chris caught 65 receptions for 1,012 yards and 10 touchdowns, leading his team to a state championship berth. Chris was named first-team All-Florida and All-Broward County. He also played basketball and was a starter as a junior when his team captured the state title.

The one thing Ohio State had in its favor was the fact that Chris' mother, Latricia, was intent on her son getting a good education. The questions she asked reminded me of the time Donna George visited the university when I was recruiting her son, Eddie George. It was clear to me that Latricia Gamble was the primary decision maker for the family. The competition for Chris' services came down to Ohio State and, no surprise, Auburn. Ultimately, Chris' mother determined Ohio State to be the best place for her son not only to continue his football career, but to get a good education.

At 6 feet 1 inch and 200 pounds, Chris proved early in his freshman year that he was indeed a special athlete. Recruited to play flanker, his diverse athletic skills prompted coaches to begin using him as a cornerback on defense in certain situations. During his freshman year in 2001, Chris played 11 games and had five receptions, including a crucial 12-yard grab at Michigan. He also had two receptions for 32 yards in the 2002 Outback Bowl. In addition, he averaged 16.4 yards per punt return on five chances.

The 2002 season marked Chris' breakout as a two-way threat. Playing cornerback for the first time against Cincinnati, he intercepted a pass in the end zone; he also deflected a pass in the corner of the end zone late in the game when the Bearcats were threatening to score a game-winning touchdown. His second interception was also made in the end zone late in a game against Wisconsin, a play that thwarted a comeback attempt by the Badgers. His third pick, which he returned for 40 yards for a touchdown, came against Penn State and was the Buckeyes only touchdown in a hard-fought 13–7 win. And his fourth interception that year came at Purdue and ended the Boilermakers' final drive in a 10–6 victory.

Offensively that season, Chris had his best game against Kent State, where he had six catches for 87 yards. He had at least three catches three other times, including Purdue, and at least one reception every game, including a 48-yard grab at Northwestern that, at the time, represented the longest of his career to that point. Chris scored his lone offensive touchdown that year on a 43-yard reverse against Indiana; he had a 93-yard touchdown return called back at Cincinnati, but still averaged 23 yards per kick return and 8.4 yards per punt return. In fact, his 56-yard kick return to open the second half at Northwestern led to a Buckeye field goal and a 17–9 lead.

It's difficult not to be impressed by Chris. Head coach Jim Tressel has also compared him with Cris Carter, whom he coached in 1984 and 1985 as a Buckeye assistant. In 2002, Chris again earned first-team All-Big Ten honors on defense, was a second-team pick on the *Sporting News* All-America team and a third-team pick by the *Associated Press*. He played 100 or more plays in each of the Buckeyes' last four games of the 2002 season including 128 at Illinois. Chris was the Buckeyes' second-leading receiver with 31 catches for 499 yards, including a 57-yard grab against Miami in the national championship game that set up a 44-yard field goal to give Ohio State a 17–7 lead. The latter reception was the longest pass play of the year for the Buckeyes. On defense in that game, Chris held highly touted receiver Andre Johnson to four receptions, with three of those coming in the first quarter. An award I know he's most proud of is being selected by his teammates, along with quarterback Craig Krenzel, as the team's most valuable player for the 2002 season.

Chris went on to earn All-Big Ten honors his junior year, declaring for the NFL draft at season's end. The No. 28 player chosen in the first round of the 2004 NFL draft by the Carolina Panthers, Chris was set to begin his second season as a pro in 2005. During his rookie season at cornerback, Chris recorded 68 tackles and six interceptions. He also forced one fumble. Carolina could realize Chris' value on the offensive side of the ball as well, and I expect good things from this special athlete in the future.

Mike Nugent: Kicker Becomes Team Captain and Icon

Mike Nugent found himself in a proverbial vacuum in early 2000 after John Cooper was fired and before Jim Tressel was hired as head football coach at Ohio State. A running back who sometimes played quarterback at Centerville High School, a perennial football powerhouse near Dayton, Ohio, Nugent, however, made a name for himself as a place kicker. I first met Mike in the summer of 1998 when he attended a kicker's camp at Ohio State and won almost every competition held. I told him at that time that I'd like to keep in touch with him, and if he did as well as I expected to be prepared to consider becoming a Buckeye. Fortunately, Mike said it was his dream since childhood to play for the Buckeyes.

Mike would have a very successful prep school career under Centerville head coach Ron Ullery. He was selected a second-team Division I *Associated Press* All-Ohio selection and first-team Western Ohio League and All-Southwest Ohio choice as a senior. In 2000, he connected on 5 of 7 field goal opportunities and was perfect on 29 of 29 PATs while also kicking a school-record 52–yard field goal. He converted 13 of 17 field goals, set a school record with 165 PATs and totaled 262 points in his four-year career. As a quarterback his senior year he threw three touchdowns and ran for seven. He served as team captain and was awarded offensive MVP honors that year. He was also a member of the National Honor Society.

Mike deserved an opportunity to fulfill his dream, but the coaching transition wasn't helping me as I could not promise him a scholarship. So, he began looking at other programs that also were recruiting him quite heavily. One of those was the University of Pittsburgh, which invited him to make an official visit.

Several weeks passed before Ohio State finally announced the hiring of Jim Tressel. At one of our first meetings as a staff, I told Jim about Nugent and he decided we should offer him a scholarship. On the day I called Mike to tell him the news, he was traveling with his parents on Interstate 70, heading to Pittsburgh for his official visit. As they were crossing a bridge from Ohio to West Virginia, I told Mike that Ohio State was prepared to offer him a scholarship. He immediately accepted without thinking, but then asked if this meant he should turn around and head home. I thought for a second, before telling him to go ahead with the visit, but to not say anything to Pitt head coach Walt Harris and recruiting coordinator Bryan Deal or he wouldn't have a very good weekend.

As he traveled back to Centerville that Sunday, Mike announced that he was coming to Ohio State. Deal, who had been an assistant of mine at Dublin High School, still jokes with me today that Mike would have committed to Pitt if I hadn't reached him via phone on that bridge. I always suspect that Mike made the right decision.

Mike would become one of the nation's best place kickers, as well as cultural phenomenon at Ohio State. Fans would roar "Nuge!" every time he took the field, as the sounds of rock star Ted Nugent's (no relation) anthem, "Stranglehold" blasted from Ohio Stadium loudspeakers.

Mike scored 48 points on 7 of 14 field goals and 27 of 29 conversions as a true freshman in 2001. He became the first Buckeye kicker to ever earn first-team All-America honors in 2002, making 25 of 28 field goals and 45 of 46 PATs for a school season record (for kickers) 120 points. He added 88 points on 16 of 19 three-pointers and all 38 extra point attempts in 2003. Mike was a consensus All-America first-team pick and recipient of the Lou Groza Award as a senior in 2004, when he hit 24 of 27 field goals, including five of at least 50 yards or more. He added 30 of 30 PATs for 102 points.

Mike holds or shares 22 Ohio State records. He finished his career with his name in the career-record books for most points scored (356), most points by a kicker (356), most field goals (72), most consecutive field goals made (24, 2001–02), most games with multiple field goals (72), most field goals of 50 yards or more (eight), and best field goal percentage (.818, 72 of 88).

Mike was selected in the second round of the 2005 NFL draft by the New York Jets, and was preparing to begin his rookie season at press time. As a coach, you like to see good things come to good people. Mike Nugent deserves all the recognition and all the rewards he has received to date. "Nuge" will long be remembered and admired by Ohio State fans, including myself.

Maurice Clarett: Ability and Baggage

His name has become synonymous for many Buckeye fans with controversy, immaturity, arrogance, disrespect and dishonor. For some, Maurice Clarett, the talented-yet-troubled running back, has also become a poster child for behavior unbecoming a college football player. It didn't start that way.

In the spring of 2002, I would have bet the house that Maurice Clarett would become one of the most laurelled running backs in the history of Ohio State, in the lineage of Howard "Hopalong" Cassidy, Vic Janowicz, Les Horvath, Keith Byars, Eddie George, and of course, Archie Griffin. Earning Mr. Football in Ohio and *USA Today's* National Offensive Player of the Year honors that fall of 2001, Maurice graduated early from Warren Harding High School in Warren, Ohio, to enroll at Ohio State in January 2002. He began working out with the team that winter and his intensity, commitment and work ethic during conditioning and subsequent spring practices rivaled that of Eddie George or Chris Spielman. By the time spring practices were concluded, this freshman sensation was clearly the player to beat for the starting running back position as we looked toward August. Nothing changed during August camp as he earned the right to start when the Buckeyes opened up the 2002 season against Texas Tech. Another factor that was impressive at the time was his personality. Very gregarious, he openly pushed and challenged veteran players to get stronger, faster and improve their skills. This kid seemed like an irresistible force of nature.

The first true freshman in Ohio State history to start at tailback in a season opener, Maurice announced his presence with authority that first game, rushing for 175 yards on 21 carries and three touchdowns as the Buckeyes manhandled the highly lauded Red Raiders, 45–21. That performance only pales in comparison to Archie Griffin's 239 yards among Ohio State freshman runners. Maurice became the first freshman since 1990, and just the second freshman in league history to be named Big Ten Offensive Player of the Week. The 6 feet, 235-pound tailback posted touchdown runs against Texas Tech of 59, 45 and two yards. He also caught four passes for 30 yards, for a total of 205 all-purpose yards. The last Big Ten freshman to win Offensive Player of the Week honors was Penn State's Zack Mills on October 29, 2001, while the only freshman to be honored after the first weekend of play was another Buckeye tailback—Robert Smith on September 10, 1990.

Interestingly, Maurice was part of an ultra-talented freshman class that included linebackers Bobby Carpenter, Mike D'Andrea and A.J. Hawk, quarterbacks Justin Zwick and Troy Smith, wide receiver Santonio Holmes, defensive back Nate Salley, and offensive lineman Nick Mangold. This class was ranked by recruiting services as the No. 2 class in the country behind the University of Texas. Interestingly, Ohio and Texas faced off for the first time in history in 2005, pitting members of these recruiting classes, who were seniors. The game was played at Ohio Stadium the evening of September 10, with Ohio State losing 25–22, in a well-played albeit heart-wrenching contest. Another interesting fact is that, of the 25 players recruited by Ohio State that year, only three did not stay with the team, including

Maurice. Of the 27 players Texas recruited that year, 10 are no longer with the team.

Maurice, even though missing a game and getting limited playing time in others because of a shoulder injury, went on to rush for 1,190 yards and 14 touchdowns that year. He also played a pivotal role in the Buckeye's 31–24 victory over the Miami Hurricanes in the Fiesta Bowl, knifing his way through the Canes' defense for a five-yard touchdown run in a second overtime. Earlier in the game, he made a great heads-up play by ripping the ball out of Sean Taylor's hands to wipe out a Miami interception.

But it is the controversy surrounding Maurice that clouds both the memories of his performances and awesome statistics. People ask me all the time when the change occurred from the hard-working Maurice witnessed in the spring and early season, to the seemingly bitter and cynical Maurice that emerged as the season wore on. Quite honestly, I don't know, but all of us saw an evolution and erosion of his personality as the season progressed. Maybe the pressure and attention got to him? Maybe he was getting bad advice from others looking to benefit from his success? Maybe the fact that he was treated much differently from other freshmen had something to do with it. How differently, you ask? Well, here's an 18-year-old kid who lived off campus instead of living in a dormitory. He also drove new cars and SUVs on a regular basis. This was not only unusual, but it steadily distanced himself from the other players.

As the season wore on, Maurice became more rude with the coaching staff, as well as our medical staff. The straw that broke the camel's back for me just happened to be witnessed by millions of people on national television. When he was replaced after fumbling the football at a critical point in the Northwestern game, he openly confronted and argued with assistant coach Tim Spencer, a former Buckeye and NFL running back, who served as the running backs coach for John Cooper and Jim Tressel. Making matters worse was the fact that Maurice was allowed to go back into the game. The 2003 season was the last for Tim Spencer as a Buckeye coach. He was offered a job by the Chicago Bears as a running backs coach, and he jumped at the opportunity.

What's more important than the problems and turmoil surrounding one player is the fact that Maurice's off-field, extracurricular antics never—I repeat, never—affected the team or its performance on game day. This includes his comments about leaving early and challenging NFL eligibility rules. It also includes when he questioned Ohio State policies and the football program's commitment to individuals when the university said it would not pay for him to leave Tempe the week leading up to the national championship game to fly to Youngstown to attend the funeral of a childhood friend. I believe the senior leadership of this team was able to maintain the strength of the unit to focus on its goal of winning a national title.

As I've told a number of people, Maurice Clarett was his own worst enemy. Here was a young man with an unbelievable amount of talent who threw away a golden opportunity, a person who took bad advice and an athlete who did not how to handle success. Maurice Clarett could have been an Ohio State legend; instead, he will probably go down as a great tragedy of the game.

Conley's Recruiting Commandments

X. Make the high school coach your ally.

If you have the high school coach on your side or keep him neutral, recruiting is much easier. The high school coach will help you get over hurdles others may encounter if you maintain good relations and are completely honest during the recruiting process.

I always enjoyed recruiting Ft. Lauderdale St. Thomas Aquinas High School. Head Coach George Smith is one of the most successful coaches in the country, and insisted that visiting college coaches keep him in the information loop regarding one of his players. I would call Coach Smith ahead of my visits to the school, and he would have transcripts and film of his players ready on my arrival. Safety Nate Salley was one of the young men I recruited from St. Thomas. I believe my relationship with Coach Smith is one of the key reasons Nate decided to attend Ohio State. Through the years, St. Thomas has placed a number of players in the college ranks, and I'm honored to call Coach Smith a friend as well as a colleague.

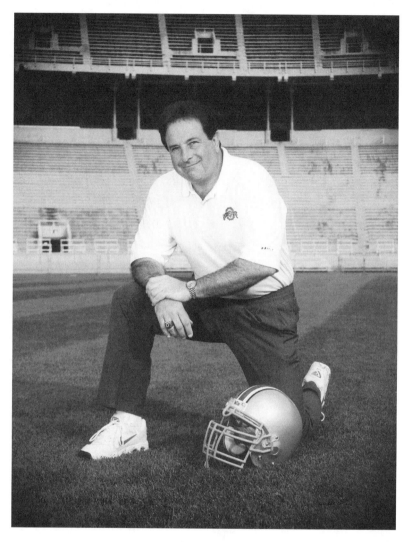

A pre-season shot prior to my last season at Ohio State in 2003.

10

The Future of Recruiting

The process of recruiting the best talent to play at the best Division I college football programs will remain as competitive as ever. The value and worth of head coaches will continue to be judged by their individual records, which is directly related to the quality of athletes they recruit and their ability to mold that talent into a successful team.

The old adage, "You can't plow the field without the horses," will remain true in the future as it is today in relation to recruiting. Off-the-field elements will also continue to be stressed and factor in a coach's legacy, as universities evaluate their return on investment. These elements include graduation rates, citizenship and alumni relations, to name a few.

Although these factors are here to stay and will always matter, the bottom line is that hiring and firing decisions will be primarily based on a coach's win-loss record. You better win more than you lose; you better have a positive percentage of wins in bowl games; and at a school like Ohio State, you better beat your archrival. At Ohio State that means the "Team Up North," as Woody referred to Michigan. Fans won't blame players or give credit to the enemy. They will blame the head coach. This is part of the joy and pain of coaching at the Division I level, and if you can't handle it, you won't last long.

College football will continue being a big-time business. Gate receipts at places like Ohio State literally fund the athletic department. Good teams bring in crowds and television contracts and that translates into higher revenues. Football programs need to produce to keep athletic programs in the black. If a university doesn't bring in the much-needed football revenues, non-revenue sports—such as golf, tennis, soccer and lacrosse, to name few—will be dropped or reduced to club status. I'm not picking on non-revenue sports, as I believe all these activities add value to the college experience. What I am talking about is the business realities of the situation.

Unfortunately, the NCAA seems to be going out of its way to bring down the quality of Division I college football. It is so concerned with equality that it is ignoring reality. The American public wants a quality product and does not want Division I college football to lose its appeal just to appease the lower-division programs. The NCAA needs to worry more about making colleges follow the rules, making the game safer and establishing sound academic standards. These were the intentions of the organization when it was formed and it should keep its nose where it belongs. If not, I predict that major Division I universities will create their own organization or super conference.

Major colleges and universities will not stand by and allow the NCAA to whittle away its primary revenue source.

As the pressure to produce good teams remains a constant in Division I football, the expectations of incoming freshmen athletes also increases. Scholarship numbers are continually decreasing and competition for these grants-in-aid will become more severe. As a result, training facilities are springing up all over the country to make athletes bigger, stronger, faster and more agile than ever. Companies such as MAX Sports Center in Dublin, Ohio, IMG in Bradenton, Florida, and Cris Carter's FAST program in Coral Springs, Florida, all have developed scientific programs to help athletes become more competitive and more skilled. These organizations have specialists in aspects of physical training not provided by the average university, college or even high school. Trainers, nutritionists, physical therapists and sports psychologists all work with athletes to raise their performance to optimum levels. National combines and camps are also springing up for athletes to showcase their abilities, and be seen by coaches and recruiters. The competition is fierce and it will continue to grow more ferocious.

As a coach, I truly believe competition in athletics or business is a good thing. There's nothing wrong with an individual working to become the best they can be in whatever arena they choose. And as long as coaches continue to teach values such as discipline, fair play, loyalty, sacrifice and teamwork, the game of football will remain the respected institution it is today. This is not a rap on baseball, but I believe football has emerged as our national pastime. The passion and pageantry surrounding college football in this country transcends socio-economic stratospheres and connects people on an emotional level, and

I think this is a good thing. This is why I vehemently disagree with Ohio State University president Karen Holbrook who, in the course of making a public apology after receiving e-mails from Texas fans complaining about being ridiculed while attending the 2005 contest, said she is working to "change the culture" of Ohio State football games. Nonsense. There are always going to be a few jerks at any public event, especially one of the magnitude of an Ohio State football game. But I know for a fact that most Buckeye fans respect Ohio State and the institution that is college football, and conduct themselves in an appropriate manner while tailgating or attending the game.

The game of football gave me a chance to make a career and have fun at something that was tough but self-fulfilling. Football gave me a chance to get an education. Football gave me the opportunity to teach important values to young people. Football gave me a chance to work with talented and dedicated coaches, athletes and administrators. Football gave me a chance to meet people from all parts of the United States and even other countries. Football gave me a chance to coach athletes and make them better than they were before. Football gave me a chance to sell recruits and their parents on an institution I truly love and respect— The Ohio State University.

I don't know if I was the best player, the best coach or the best recruiter, but I do know I gave it my very best effort. That's all a coach can ask of his players and that's all he can ask of himself.

Conley's Recruiting Commandments

XI. Parents must trust you.

As the coach that is recruiting their son, parents see you fulfilling their roles once their child leaves home. They must have faith that you will treat their son as your son if he decides to attend your university.

I always introduced recruits and their parents to former team doctor Dr. John Lombardo, and team trainers Doug Calland and Bill Davis. This way, the recruit and his parents understood that the health and safety of our athletes is of vital importance. In fact, I developed such a close relationship with Dr. Lombardo that I decided to join him at MAX Sports Center in Dublin, Ohio, after retiring from Ohio State.

This painting, created by Moments Productions was presented to the coaches after we won the National Championship game. Yes, that's me, below the "O" of Ohio State and above Head Coach Jim Tressel.

The "All-Conley" Team

I have been asked many times to identify the best player or players with whom I played, coached or recruited. It's a loaded request, a no-win position and something that can be mind-boggling, to say the least. Consider the criteria that could be used and, arguably, all justified. Do you go by raw statistics, key performances, number of rewards, or years and accolades earned playing beyond college in the NFL? Some would argue the latter standard proves the prepotency of an athlete. I can neither unequivocally disagree nor agree.

I think back to the years I played as a Buckeye and truly believe some of Ohio State's greatest players were my teammates. Few could argue that some of the best offensive linemen played at that time. Outland and Lombardi winner John Hicks, who came in second place for the Heisman Trophy, was as athletic a lineman as any to play the game of football. The great Ohio State tradition of offensive linemen attracted players such as Dave Foley, Rufus Mayes, Alan Jack and Tom DeLeone. Hard running and physical backs like Jim Otis and John Brockington, or fleet-of-foot Leo Hayden and Larry Zelina made the running game at Ohio State the envy of the nation. The premiere quarterback of this era was All-American Rex Kern, who was as much of a running threat as a passing threat. When Rex would air it out, tight end Jan White or wide out Bruce Jankowski were the targets.

During that era, we were equally known for great defensive players. Woody Hayes had a knack for knowing where to place the talent he recruited. He would sometimes match a player to a different position from one year to the next, like tight end/linebacker Stan White, depending on the needs of the team and talent in a particular position.

Coming out of high school and playing linebacker my first year at Ohio State, I marveled at the talent of other players at my position, like Dirk Worden, Mark Stier, Doug Adams, and the previously mentioned Stan White. They weren't big by today's standards, but they could run and they could hit. A couple of young linebackers of that time who would eventually make their mark as Buckeyes were Randy Gradishar and Rick Middleton. The defensive front was equally impressive with Outland and Lombardi winner Jim Stillwagon leading the way. However, players such as George Hasnerhrol, Mark Debevc and Dave Whitfield were some of the best at their positions.

Defensively, some argue that the cream of the Buckeye crop of that era played in the secondary. It's important to remember that, at that time, defensive backs were more like linebackers. The harder you hit, the more your talents were recognized. That's why

Buckeye great Jack Tatum was king of the hill. He could run like a deer and hit like a freight train. He also had a great supporting cast in guys such as Ted Provost, Mike Sensibaugh and Tim Anderson. These are just a few of the stars of my playing days. They were teammates and friends who were respected as some of the best collegiate players of the time. Everything is relative to that era, so to compare these athletes with the players of today is impossible in my view. Today, football players are bigger, stronger and faster than ever. Let there be no doubt, however, I truly believe these players could play the game today and play it well.

Again, I have pondered the question, "Who are the best players I have been associated with while coaching at Ohio State?" Under three head coaches and after 17 seasons, is it truly feasible to come up with an "All-Conley Team?" To identify and place the great Buckeyes I have coached and recruited on an All-Star team would be quite a challenge. From 1984 to 1987 and 1991 to 2003, we had a Who's Who of college football talent at Ohio State. I have Heisman, Outland, Lombardi, Walter Camp, Belitnikoff, Jim Thorpe, Remington, Ray Gray and Groza award winners, and a smorgasbord of talent from which to choose. Can it be done? I will attempt to provide a list of nominees from the best of the best, but I will rely on your help to select the "All-Conley Team," so put on your thinking cap. After careful consideration, log onto: *www.CoachBillConley.com* to make your selections.

The players on the "quick list" were either two-year starters, All-Big Ten, or All-America selections. Many went on to play and continue to play in the National Football League. I truly hope not to offend anyone by leaving them off the list, but a final cut had to be made.

The "All-Conley Offense" will consist of one tight end, five linemen, one quarterback, two running backs and two (yes, only two) wide receivers. Defensively, there will be three linebackers, four defensive linemen and four defensive backs. Rounding out the "All-Conley Team" will be three specialists—a punter, a place kicker and a long snapper. Remember, these players have played in the aforementioned 17-year span I had the privilege to coach and recruit at Ohio State. The players are listed in random order, and the choices must come from these nominees:

"All-Conley Team" Offensive Nominees

Linemen
Juan Porter
Rob Murphy
Orlando Pace
Kurt Murphy
Korey Stringer
Bob Maggs
Rob Sims
Adriane Clarke
Ben Gilbert
Shane Olivea
Nick Mangold
Alex Stepanovich
LeCharles Bentley
Eric Gohlstin
Jim Lachey
Alan Kline
Dave Monnot
Len Hartman
LeShun Daniels
Kirk Lowdermilk
Tyson Walter
Joe Staysniak
Tim Moxley

Rory Graves
Jeff Uhlenhake
Scott Zalenski
Greg Zackeroff
Paul Long
Jason Winrow
Bryce Bishop

Receivers
Mike Lanese
Terry Glenn
Dimetrious Stanley
Michael Jenkins
Brian Stablein
Dee Miller
Joey Galloway
Cris Carter
Chris Sanders
David Boston
Reggie Germany
Ken-Yon Rambo
Drew Carter

Backs
Robert Smith
Carlos Snow
Keith Byars
Jamar Martin
Eddie George
Vince Workman
Raymont Harris
Maurice Clarett
Michael Wiley
Pepe Pearson
George Cooper
Jeff Cothran
Matt Keller

Tight Ends
Darnell Sanders
Ed Taggart
Ben Hartsock
Cedrick Saunders
Ricky Dudley
John Lumpkin
D.J. Jones

Quarterback
Mike Tomczak
Jim Karsatos
Greg Frey
Bobby Hoying
Steve Bellisari
Stanley Jackson
Joe Germaine
Craig Krenzel

"All-Conley Team" Defensive Nominees

Linemen
Jason Simmons
Matt Finkes
Ryan Pickett
Tim Anderson
Dan Wilkinson
Will Smith
Darryl Lee
Mike Vrabel
Simon Fraser
Rodney Bailey
Darrion Scott
Luke Fickell
Mike Collins
Winfield Garnett
Brent Johnson
Matt Bonhaus
Mike Sullivan
Mike McCray
Eric Kumerow
Byron Lee
Alonzo Spellman

Greg Smith
Mark Williams

Linebackers
Pepper Johnson
Matt Wilhelm
A.J. Hawk
Na'il Diggs
Steve Tovar
Larry Kolic
Lorenzo Styles
Andy Katzenmoyer
Ryan Miller
Chris Spielman
Robert Reynolds
Courtland Bullard
Greg Bellisari
Derek Isaman
Jerry Rudzinski
Craig Powell
Joe Cooper

Backs

Damon Moore	Dustin Fox	Shawn Springs
Chris Gamble	Rob Kelly	Will Allen
Ahmed Plummer	Greg Rogan	Derek Ross
Roger Harper	Marlon Kerner	Bryan Cook
Sonny Gordon	Donnie Nickey	Zack Dumas
Chico Nelson	Nate Clements	David Brown
Tim Walton	Nate Salley	William White
Cie Grant	Michael Doss	Terry White
Antoine Winfield	Gary Berry Jr.	Ty Howard

"All-Conley Team" Specialists Nominees

Place Kickers	Punters	Long Snappers
Dan Stultz	Brent Bartholomew	Kevin Houser
Rich Spangler	Andy Groom	Kyle Andrews
Tim Williams	Tom Tupa	Jim Borchers
Mike Nugent	Scott Terna	Dean Kreuzer
Matt Frantz	B.J. Sander	Doug Whitmer
Josh Jackson		
Pat O'Morrow		

You now see how difficult it is for me to choose the best of the best. Think of the wide receiver position alone. How do you pick just two? Everyone remembers the big play makers like Michael Jenkins's fourth-down touchdown grab against Purdue during the 2002 national championship season. What about Cris Carter's one-hand snare in the 1985 Citrus Bowl against Brigham Young or Terry Glenn's breakaway touchdown against Notre Dame in 1995? What about the steady, sure hands of Mike Lanese, Dee Miller or David Boston. Can you pick just two?

Things don't get easier on the defensive side of the equation. Just thinking about selecting an All-Star linebacking corps makes your head spin. Several Buckeye linebackers will go down as some of the greatest to ever play the game of football. Can anyone argue against leaving off Pepper Johnson, who had many years of NFL success after leaving Ohio State? What about A.J. Hawk, whose potential we're only beginning to see? Then there's Chris Spielman, who many people put in a category by himself, including me. Counter that with the great team leadership of a Greg Bellisari and you have a never-ending debate. But let's add to the mix Andy Katzenmoyer, whose NFL career was cut short, but has unmatched collegiate statistics and highlights. What about the great athlete linebackers and ends, such as Na'il Diggs, Mike Vrabel or Will Smith? I'm sure former Miami Hurricane quarterback Ken Dorsey would place a vote for Matt Wilhelm, whose brutal, overtime sack in the national championship game put Dorsey in another dimension, literally, and set up Cie Grant's game-ending play.

Examining running backs doesn't make it any easier. Heisman Trophy winner Eddie George owns one spot, but how can you pick just one other to join him? Would you pick a big back, such as Keith Byars or Jamar Martin, or would you choose the speedy Robert Smith or Pepe Pearson? What about getting the best of both worlds with Maurice Clarett, or do his personal issues cloud your analytical abilities?

The toughest position of all from which to choose is the defensive secondary. To pick four from a list of some of college football's all-time best is no easy undertaking. One of the fastest Buckeyes of all time was Shawn Springs, who is a strong candidate to break into the starting lineup of the "All-Conley

Team." Could you leave off Jim Thorpe Award winner Antoine Winfield or three-time All-Big Ten selection Michael Doss? William White played in the NFL for over a dozen years and Chris Gamble never left the field as a corner and a wide out. Damon Moore has a school-record two interception returns for touchdowns and Nate Clements was feared by the opposition as punt returner. How do you pick only four? Who do you leave off a list of starters?

This is why I need your help. I've come to the conclusion that I can't come to a conclusion. Maybe I'm not as fearless as John Madden, but he picks players only from a given year. Besides, he doesn't have to live in Columbus, Ohio, and most of these guys still know where to find me. Believe me, I'm not outrunning any of them, either.

On a serious note, how do you pick an All-Star starting lineup from this list of players? The other thing to remember is that all of these players had great supporting casts around them, and team chemistry dictates both personal and team performance. As a coach you remember it all, the great plays, the great players and the great teams. It would be unfair for me to select an "All-Conley Team" at this point, but I might be able to do it in the future. But for now, I'm content knowing that I had the honor and privilege of being part of an era of Buckeye greats.

In the end, it's not the championship rings, trophies, plaques and watches that mean so much to a coach. It's the faces of the young men you see in these objects of success. The faces I see in my mind are not only the "great" players, but all of those players who did their jobs in a way that permitted great players to do great things. This includes all the scout team players who made our starters better. I've known many a scout player who could be a starter for other Division I programs. But they chose to be a Buckeye, and that makes them special. Each player on a team is the same in a coach's eye because they are all there with the same purpose in mind . . . to win together. That's what makes a team sport like football special, and what makes a coach a coach.

Index

Page numbers in bold type refer to photographs

About J.C. Phillips

Jeff Phillips is an award-winning journalist and business writer who owns a Circleville, Ohio-based marketing company. During his 20-year career, Phillips' work has been recognized by numerous industry organizations, including the Associated Press, United Press International, the Cleveland Press Club, Central Ohio Society of Professional Journalists, Advertising Federation of America and International Association of Business Communicators.

Phillips is also an assistant varsity football coach in charge of running backs and defensive line at Bexley High School in Bexley, Ohio (a Columbus suburb). He works with his brother, head coach Tom Phillips, and offensive coordinator Greg Frey, a former Ohio State quarterback and captain, who was a three-year starter between 1988 and 1990.

Phillips is a native of that "State Up North," originally hailing from Grand Rapids, Michigan. His family ultimately settled in New Middletown, Ohio (near Youngstown), where his parents, Glenn and Patricia Phillips, still reside.

The eldest of four brothers from a sports-rich family, Phillips' youngest brother, Doug, is head football coach at Salem High School in Salem, Ohio (near Alliance). In the early 1990s, Doug Phillips served as a graduate assistant coach at Youngstown State University under current Ohio State head coach Jim Tressel.

Jeff Phillips and his wife and native Buckeye, Kari Hammer-Phillips, reside in Stoutsville, Ohio, where they breed and exhibit Boxers under the kennel name Logan Elm Boxers.